Journey to My Soul

Following Divine Navigation

Terri Lynn

Balboa Press books may be ordered through booksellers or by contacting:

Balboa Press
A Division of Hay House
1663 Liberty Drive
Bloomington, IN 47403
www.balboapress.com
1-(877) 407-4847

ISBN: 978-1-4525-4505-9 (sc)
ISBN: 978-1-4525-4506-6 (hc)
ISBN: 978-1-4525-4504-2 (e)
Library of Congress Control Number: 2011963720

Printed in the United States of America

Balboa Press rev. date: 1/25/2012

To my loving sons,
Jerome and Dan.
Thank you for the joy!

Acknowledgments

My love and appreciation go to my fabulous sisters, Rosemary Gulati, Eileen Ferrero, and Anne Rotondo, for all their love, support, and friendship throughout my life, and especially for their vital feedback during the development of this book. A special thank you to, Rosemary, for her expertise in editing along with the many hours she spent with me in reviewing this project. There are no words to express how truly grateful I am. Also, thanks to my children, Jerome, Theresa, and Dan, for their continuous love and support.

Much gratitude goes to my friend and co-worker, Keith Rentchshler, who tagged me with the nickname, Fortune Cookie, which ignited my passion and inspired me to write this book. Thank you to, Joan Blake Kirsch, for her friendship, coaching, and expert photography. Thanks to my lifelong friend, Lyn Fitzpatrick Foster, for her unconditional love and support, and to my friends Beth DeSabatino, Paul Schradieck, Carole Phelps, Fran Richman, and Joan Phillips, for their loving support, and many thanks to all of my supporters in my dance family. A big thank you to my friend Pat McDonnell, who was with me when the wave of awakening revealed the meaning of my dream, for sharing her insights, listening to me without judgment, and most of all for holding her breath. I believe you can exhale now, Pat, the book is finished.

My deepest gratitude extends to, Dr. Brian Capaldi, of Peak Potential Wellness Center, and Jeff Myers, of Universal Massage Arts for their professional assistance during my painful transition. Also, thanks to the staff at Balboa Press for guiding me in completion of this project.

Introduction

Where's Happiness?

What does happiness mean to you? Are you content with your life? Do you feel that you are where you should be? The very fact that you are reading these words indicates that there must be a message in these pages that you are meant to discover. That is how my life has always worked. There's a universal connection that binds all things, a spiritual guidance that provides us the answers we seek.

If you are searching for a "magical" solution to a problem in your own life, you may not find it here. However, you may discover in these pages just how to find a magical solution to your happiness *within yourself.* Following a path of self-discovery is exactly how my inner barriers broke down to create the life of my dreams. Taking the time to look inside myself changed my life in the best way possible. Do you know what you hold deep within your soul? Have you looked inside yourself? If you have not, you may be quite surprised to find the answers you have been seeking.

Today, my story is a happily ever after tale. However, my success story began in the middle of a nightmare, a sad, horrific nightmare. Once upon a time, long, long ago, my dream of motherhood and family life came true. Very quickly, however, that dream shattered, like a mirror broken into a thousand jagged pieces, beyond repair. My life fragmented into unrecognizable flashes of horror. But that is a story for another time.

Now is the time for me to tell the tale of how my decision to be happy, no matter what, helped me survive, and how my fight to live through the sadness moved me forward. I learned that keeping a positive focus and living a life dedicated to prayer, gratitude and discipline helped me discover many miracles along the way. The greatest miracle came to light only after my journey deep within. This book is about my successful journey of getting to the positive side of pain.

If you are a person like my friend Dave who has difficulty with the concept of God, you still may find a message in these pages. Just replace the term God with the universe, the source, Higher Power, higher self, energy or whatever works for you. Please come along and see how my life transforms from living on welfare amid shattered dreams to a successful career in the automobile business. Find out how a new dream awakens in me and ignites my passion for success.

After a few years in car sales my career skyrockets. It isn't all fun and games. There are a few upsets along the way, and many long hours to endure. However, I reach my goal of becoming a sales manager in less than seven years. My choice to be happy brought me more success than I ever imagined, a beautiful home, a free car with gas and free health insurance.

Traveling all over the US and Europe for free, perks I earn through sales rankings and contests, my life continually improves. By 2004, my income peaks at $170,000.00. This upscale life, however, is not the life of my dreams. It is a fantastic life with security and prestige, but my spiritual path calls me to go deeper.

In the mid to late nineties when I become aware of my own limiting beliefs, those thoughts that hold people back from reaching their full potential, I awake to new possibilities. I am happy with the money I earn, but the effort it requires carries a toll - working nights and weekends with never two days off in a row; I had bought into the belief that the only way to earn money is to work hard and put in long hours.

Realizing that my work ethic serves me well, I think there must be another career path that will provide me more freedom. I start digging deeper to find a new direction for my life. However, I do not know how to change a limiting belief, so the idea just stays in my consciousness. I have no time to figure out how to make a change at this point.

In my new awareness is the understanding that my limiting belief is holding me back in very much the same way as a limiter that had been applied to my children's go-cart engine years ago. My young boys had a professional go-cart, but the engine had more power than they could handle. A limiter was applied to the engine to cut the power in half. It limited the output of the engine. That is exactly what a limiting belief does. It reduces the power within and holds back the limitless possibilities in life.

Follow me and see how my beliefs do finally change and what discoveries come to light that release my true passion. Uncovering another limiting belief reveals how half my life has been lived in "limp" mode, not using all cylinders, even with all my success. What I found inside me allows me to let go of yet another limiting belief that held me back, having always believed it to be a fact, and unchangeable.

It's through my understanding of my life's journey that I'm able to bring to light my discoveries in the hope of helping someone else, possibly you. Spending many years choosing happiness, no matter what, gives me the insight to see how this choice changed my life. Having gratitude for my life, even when it is a horror story, and not the life I planned, gives me more joy today than I ever imagined.

In 2009, my own healing power cures a thyroid condition without medication. I will share with you how I conquer my physical condition amidst all those who said it could not be done. Just be certain that all things are possible with faith, and without limiting beliefs. I am so happy and grateful I finally learn to listen to myself.

In letting go of all limiting beliefs I am able to take the plunge with both feet and make the commitment to write this book. I now believe I can do anything I put my mind to. My message to you is that if I can do it, so can you. The first step is just to be happy right where you are, even if it is not where you wish to be. The fast track to any goal is to start being happy now, without excuses. Happiness will take you to your goal faster.

The information in this book is my personal journey and how my faith, coupled with positive action, changes my life. Putting in the time and effort to discover what lies within me helps unlock the blocks. My hope is that by revealing how my blocks are released you also may learn how to uncover whatever is possibly holding you back.

I'll also share with you some poems I've written along the way and hope they inspire you to plunge into your own soul. You see, I've always been a writer. I have always written poems, songs, prayers, and stories but I did not believe I could make a living from it; another limiting belief. Do you have any limiting beliefs of which you are aware?

Please come with me and see how my journey inward has many surprises. Learn how I change my beliefs and am able to let go of my past pain. Without awareness, nothing can change. I discover true miracles do happen. Many times we just don't wait long enough for them to appear. My life miracle only took twenty-five years to discover. Once this miracle is revealed I gain a new perspective with a bird's eye view that allows me to see the magic and miracles that followed me my whole life.

The discovery takes me by surprise because I wasn't looking for a miracle. Twenty-five years ago I used to say, "I need a miracle to fix my life!" I'm so glad I did not sit around waiting for it. Instead, I focused on all that was good in my life and not what was missing, and believe me, there was much missing.

My positive action in troubled times created the miracle I'm living today, with help and guidance from above, or perhaps as I see it now, Divine help from within. Within us is the connection we need to feel complete; we just need to tune-in and seek the power.

Are you waiting for a miracle? Waiting for something outside yourself to change you? This is your life, and it's a wonderful gift. Please, make the time for your own self-discovery. You will find all the answers you need and may even uncover your own miracle. Here's hoping you do.

Nature's Tide

The feelings come and the feelings go
Just as the tides so we too flow
We can ride the wave or fight the tow
For this is your life; it is your show

As simple as that this life seldom seems
Much more complex, not by any means
The choice is ours, that is, we are free
To accept what life offers, or choose to flee

Place a value on life above worldly possessions
And then take a place in nature's procession
In our lives we have our own seasons to show
Like the trees in winter, lives must be let go

As the human race continues, lives come and go
And it's certainly clear that we continue to grow
Our purpose on earth is not our own
Not to discover it is to remain unknown

Summer 1980 left: Jerome age 8, Danny age 6 1/2

Chapter 1
What You Think Matters

How do you view the world? Are you a glass half full person or do you subscribe to the glass half empty theory? How we view the world really does impact our lives. One friend of mine has the opinion that if she empties her glass at the end of each day, she will get more in her glass the next day; another friend tells me that her glass is so full that it spills over the top!

So which philosophy will bring more happiness to you? How does your belief system serve you? The creative power of the mind is beyond what we can even imagine, and most of us aren't even aware of what we are thinking. How crazy is that? What you think matters.

Every thought is a seed, a spark of creative energy. One brief thought does not carry much power; however, the same thought over and over produces results, even if we are not aware of what we are creating. This is why it is important how you view the world, what you think, and especially what you believe. Are you happy? On a scale of one to ten, where do you fit? What do you do to increase your level of happiness? Do you believe you are able to control your own happiness?

There is an old saying that "ignorance is bliss," that to be happy means to be stupid or unaware, but studies have shown just the opposite. Happy people make better employees, are more resilient, have a broader scope when faced with problem solving, possess a better immune system, bounce back faster, and the list goes on. So why are more people not focused on being happier?

We each hold the power to happiness in our own hands. Daily circumstances may vary the degree at times, but the strongest control lies within us. We are all different and what makes me happy may not be the formula for you. Only you have the power to increase your own level of happiness.

Faith gives me much happiness. Believing in a power outside of myself helps me see that all things are possible when I let go of the control. My life gives witness to the power of God and the way happiness can develop from a conscious decision to be happy, even in the midst of hell. Faith is a huge piece of my happiness.

Gratitude multiplies happiness more than anything. Appreciation can only add value; just like math, positives add and negatives subtract. Setting goals gives us focus, but being happy and grateful takes us wherever we want to go in life faster. Being grateful makes you feel good, and when you feel good, good things happen. Making a gratitude list is a great way to increase happiness over time. A gratitude journal works wonders for me. Once a month, once a week, once a day, whatever effort is put in is a plus. The more focus put on good things the better life feels, and gratitude breeds happiness. It takes discipline and training to change old patterns, but it is well worth it. Once the effort is made to get to the top level of happiness, it is much easier to maintain.

To reach my top level of happiness I meditate, exercise, follow a healthy diet, and get sufficient sleep. Meditating decreases stress, improves health, and helps me to become more aware of my thoughts.

Meditation is definitely a catalyst that transforms my life into the life of my dreams. Good diet and exercise make a body healthy. Healthier is happier, for sure. Getting adequate sleep goes without saying. So how many things do you do to boost your own happiness? What are you willing to do?

When happiness comes first, everything in life is enhanced - *everything!* But so many people don't make the time to enhance their own happiness. Many folks are just stuck, putting all their efforts into getting by when they could be enjoying so much more. Are you stuck?

Many people I know just focus on the negatives, stuck in anger, bitterness, resentment, or being a victim. Whatever negatives you may be holding on to, please for your own sake, let them go. Even if the anger is directed at someone else, that anger only takes away from the person holding it. Here's an example:

> *Sitting at my desk one afternoon a young gentleman entered my office. He worked part-time answering phones at the BMW center where I am the Sales Manager. He handed me a little piece of paper from his fortune cookie he had eaten for lunch that read, "Focus on the positive and you will flourish." He says to me, "This reminded me of you."*
>
> *His thoughtfulness really put a smile on my face. When he started working at the dealership, he was so negative and down about life. His father, who had the same name as he, took his social security number and ruined his credit before he was eighteen years of age. This young man was so bitter and angry about this betrayal. He barely knew his father and just had hate spewing out of him about how his life was ruined. The anger showed in his demeanor.*
>
> *He was a very smart, polite young man, but he believed there was no hope for his future. He was all doom and gloom. Every*

day I talked with him a little to try to shine some light and get him to see a brighter picture. Months passed and I got nowhere; he was certain his life would suck forever! Finally, one day as he was ranting on about how it really doesn't matter what he does, his future is ruined, blah, blah, blah. I got so angry and said in a forceful manner, "What if you get to the end of your life and you realize you were wrong? What then? It will be too late! Isn't it better to think of all the possibilities that may be ahead then to doom yourself before you get started? What if you are WRONG? What if you are WRONG! I said again. Use your imagination to think of something good that might happen!" and with that being said, I walked off.

Something happened that day. My anger got to him. I see it as a true miracle. His whole personality changed. A door opened that allowed him to see the possibility of a great future. He realized that the horrible situation he was living with would pass one day. He also awoke to the fact that his anger was hurting him, not his father. Once this young gentleman let go of his anger, his whole expression changed. Everyone could see the difference in him immediately. His whole attitude shifted to the positive side. He became more alive and focused on his future. He began filing for grants and scholarships, and sure enough, he got what he needed. He became so grateful to me for helping him see the possibilities, and he made sure everyone knew how I was the one that helped him make the shift.

Even after he stopped working with me, he occasionally popped in to get a pep talk or to let me know how he was doing. So, on that particular day when he gave me his fortune cookie message, it made me feel good knowing that I made a difference in his life. It is also one of those messages that the universe sends out all the time, and I call these messages, Godsends.

The positive message from that fortune cookie is a good daily reminder for me to keep a positive focus. I tape the message on my computer keyboard. Life on the job is pretty hectic, and that little message I see every day makes me feel good. Over the next several years that fortune cookie message gives me a positive focus whenever I need it. And believe me when I say, "I need it often."

That incident occurred a few years ago. In the end, the young man that awakened to new possibilities, and delivered the fortune cookie message to me, ended up giving me as much, if not more, than I had given him. You get back what you give...and often times more.

The BMW center where I work is getting more chaotic with each passing day, not so much due to business but because of a dysfunctional hierarchy. Four General Managers have been replaced in a two year period. Working with a new General Manager is always a major adjustment for all employees, but especially managers.

The owners are not hands-on people because they travel a great deal, but all is fine until they purchase a second BMW center in 2003, and business takes a little dip. To me it appears that they have become nervous. They do have a lot riding on two BMW franchises. They begin making change after change; to me and other employees their actions feel frantic.

After the purchase of the second franchise they begin to handle business from a distance so to keep an eye on things from afar. This seems to make things a little crazy. When it comes to the business, in my opinion, things would have been better if they were in office full-time or allowed the person in charge to make the decisions.

Both owners are wonderful, fun people to be around, and I enjoy working for them. The Mr. is easy to get along with, has an obvious love of life, and lives with exuberance. They lead an active life but always find time for charity events. They are true pillars in the community.

Because the owners' extravagant lifestyle keeps them away from the two centers much of the time, they hire a personal secretary to keep them filled in on the daily happenings. The personal secretary is a very sweet woman who has worked in several different departments over the past several years. She knows everyone in the workplace and is liked by all because of her lovely, caring disposition. Her job is to let them know *EVERYTHING* that goes on. We nickname the secretary 'the spy:' she fills them in by phone on the day-to-day happenings. This communication creates a full three-ring circus.

'The spy' lives in fear of losing her job, as many employees do at this time, because heads roll constantly. The employees term the firing of people as the 'revolving door.' So, 'the spy' has reason to have concern. Therefore, out of fear she reports every little detail, and some things would be better omitted. When confronted about her daily reports, she explains her fear to me, and I understand.

My current boss, the General Manager, does not have sales experience and appears to have no idea of how to handle the owners. He was previously service and parts director for all the stores and did an excellent job. I had worked with him for a few years prior to him becoming my boss. He is congenial, but from what I see, he has far too much responsibility for one person to handle.

In March of 2005, the GM calls me to his office. The owners are off on their yacht and have called in because the Mrs. suggests we serve hot dogs during our sale on Saturday. So my boss says to me, "I will get 'B' to get the hot dog cart out and clean it up. He can handle the hot dogs." I say cheerfully, "Whatever the Mrs. wants, the Mrs. gets!"

As I head back toward my office, there are three salesmen lined up outside my door. The first salesman says, "Mr. Jones placed his order, and I need to know the timeframe for delivery." So I check the availability sheet and answer the question. The next salesman needs a price for a phone customer. At that moment the GM calls me on the phone. He tells me there's an issue with the hot dogs and can I return to his office. I tell him, "I'll be there as soon as I can. I'm working a deal." The salesman in front of me is new. He tells me that he needs a price for a car in stock. I ask him who the phone customer is, and he gives me a name. I ask him where did he live, did he test-drive the car, did he set an appointment, is this the car the customer wants to buy or is he shopping other makes? He has no answers for me.

As I glance down, I happen to see the fortune cookie message that is taped on my computer, *Focus on the positive and you will flourish.* I take a deep breath and say, "I know you are really excited and want to sell a car." He agrees and answers in an excited frenzy that we have the exact car the customer wants in stock. I tell him that his enthusiasm is great. (Someone else comes to my door. I look up and ask if it can wait a few minutes, and I proceed.) I ask him what his job is here. He looks puzzled and says, "Sell cars?" "Yes," I reply, "but I think you are forgetting one thing." (Another interruption, the lot attendant comes rushing in and lets me know there's a damaged car coming off the truck. "I'll be there in a few.")

"Any idea what you forgot," I ask. "I did get his phone number!" he says with enthusiasm. "The one important thing you forgot is that price does not sell the car. You need to get more information so you know that the client understands the brand value and what he is getting for his money. What if he's looking at a Honda or a Toyota and is just looking at the price? Does he know that our car has a better value, free maintenance, a better warranty? Did he drive our car? Maybe our shopper does know all about BMW, but you'll never know if you don't ask."

"There's so much more to selling cars than just price. I need to go and take care of a few things. Why don't you call him with the MSRP price and get some more information. Ask him if he'd like to take a test drive. Ask him if he is shopping any other makes. Try to set an appointment with him. Since we have the exact car, ask if you can take it to him. If it's only price he wants, ask him what price does he have in mind?" The young salesman still looks so excited and replies, "Thank you!" As he was walking away, I tell him to keep up the good attitude! With his bubbling enthusiasm, somehow I know he will sell that car, and that is what he does.

As I walk out of my office, another salesman tells me that he needs me to locate a car ASAP. I excitedly reply, "You sell them, and I'll get them!" Just leave the locator sheet on my desk. "Great job," I say to him enthusiastically. He shakes his head and laughingly says, "I don't know how you stay so upbeat with all that goes on in your office, thanks."

I return to the GM's office to tell him that I'm needed outside and I'll be back. It is never pleasant to handle a new car that arrives with damage because it creates stress for all parties involved. On my way back I run into 'B,' and he's very upset. He speaks with a heavy accent and when he's upset, he's difficult to understand, a bit comical actually. He's ranting that he's not cooking hot dogs on Saturday in the freezing cold. The GM walks by looking very frustrated. He says to me, "Ask 'M' if she will serve the hot dogs if I can figure out who will cook them." I agree to ask her and head back to my office. 'M' helps the sales team with clerical work.

Back in my office the work is piled high. I have five voice mails and another few people waiting, plus the car to locate, and a report to finish. The first line of duty is a salesman who wants to know if I will take a deal he is working. I check the numbers and say, "Great job!" The second salesman needs help working some numbers on a deal. As I am working figures on a lease, 'M' walks by and I ask her about the hot dogs. She replies that she's not comfortable handling food and would rather not.

As I continue working on the figures for the lease, the body shop calls about the damaged car. As I hang up the phone, a customer arrives with an issue that needs to be resolved. I send the salesman out with his lease figures and turn my attention to the customer. By the time we resolve his concern, we are both laughing. Most customer issues are easy enough to handle; I just do the right thing.

By now, two more salespeople need assistance. Do you see the picture? It's a non-stop pace. That is why the fortune cookie message taped to my computer helps me stay positive. I actually love the pace of the job. It is pure action, and I enjoy it. It is the other nonsense that has nothing to do with being productive that takes the pleasure away for me.

When the GM discovers that 'M' does not wish to serve hot dogs, he rolls his eyes. He's angry now and blurts out that he has better things to do than this bullshit! I ask him "Why don't you just tell the Mrs. that the hot dogs are not a good idea for the March sale? It's too cold; we can have them when the weather gets warmer and be done with it. She's a reasonable woman. Did you tell her the temperature will be in the 30's on Saturday? When they left the weather was much warmer. The hot dog cart isn't for indoor use. You are in charge, right?"

He looks at me as if I am crazy for suggesting that he take control of the situation. He doesn't have the guts to suggest common sense to the owners. He is their yes man, and the circus is just starting. (Send in the clowns)

The HR woman shares an office with the GM. She walks into the office with the owner's spy when the GM and I are discussing the hot dog issue. She can see that he's upset. He then tells her about the hot dogs, how 'B' doesn't want to cook them, and 'M' does not want to serve them. The three of them converse as if this were a matter of major importance and allow it to take precedence over all other business. (The ring master joins the clowns and announces the next act.)

Disbelieving what I am seeing, I scurry out of there. As I head back to my office, there are many more items to handle. I call and make arrangements for a dealer trade. Then I arrange to send a check to the dealer and hire a truck to pick up the sold car. I inform the salesman that I located his sold car, and it will be here in the morning. We both do a little happy dance. I make sure we celebrate each sale. This is the reason we are here. This is how we get paid.

Another manager in the company walks into my office and asks what's going on with the hot dogs? He heard 'the spy' on the phone giving details to the Mrs. I look up and say, "The Mrs. wants hot dogs for the sale on Saturday. Our fearless leader doesn't have the nerve to say what a ridiculous idea that is." He responds, "That's why the owners made him the GM! Yes them to death!" (Now, the jugglers arrive to join the circus.)

The next day I receive a phone call from the owner himself. He is upset because 'M' refuses to serve the hot dogs. I report to him that I only casually asked her, and she said, "I'd rather not." I tell him it's not really a big deal and explain that the whole episode is blown out of proportion. I tell him I will serve the hot dogs. He feels disciplinary action is required. I ask him to please wait until he gets back so we can talk in person. It is agreed. (Now comes the flying trapeze act, and there is no net!)

By now everyone is up in arms about the hot dogs. 'M' hears from 'the spy' that the owners are upset with her and she may even be fired. She goes back to the HR and GM's office and is very upset. She's crying and ranting, "I am not a food handler! Hot dogs gag me! I know my rights and I cannot be fired for this. I am not a food server!" She calls out sick the next day because she was so upset that she didn't sleep all night. Immediately 'the spy' calls to report. The whole episode escalates. (Elephants are now doing their tricks with the jugglers and clowns in the center ring.)

The owner's personal driver now enters the show. There are at least five key people, including me, tied up for hours in the GM's office talking about the hot dog fiasco. It is such a colossal waste of time and money. You might think that the hot dogs are a matter of national security. As I leave their office, it is hard for me to comprehend what had just happened. Looking back now it seems even more ridiculous, but it is all true. This sort of craziness continues for four straight days. (It is now a full three-ring circus with plenty of hot dogs!)

The day of the sale we brought in a tabletop hot dog cooker. I serve. We have three customers eat hot dogs.

The hot dog circus is only one of the crazy, dysfunctional tales of this time in my life, a constant distraction from the job I love. And it is that little reminder to *Focus on the positive and you will flourish* that keeps giving back to me in a big way. Having a positive focus and maintaining thoughts that serve the life I desire are crucial to my success. Do your thoughts serve you to create the life you desire? Are you aware of what you are thinking? Are you aware of what you are creating? Learning how to have a positive focus has helped transform my life, and it goes back to when I was a young child.

From the time I was six years old I've had a positive attitude, even in my darkest days. It stems from a lesson my mother was brilliant enough to teach me as a child. When I was just one year old my parents opened a gift shop that my mother managed. When she was at work, my main caretakers were my grandfather who lived with us, and my sister Kathleen who was a teenager at the time. I was the youngest of five girls so I was always in good hands.

Love is the keyword I use to describe the home where I grew up. My sister Rosemary always says that as each child enters a family that child changes the family dynamic. By the time I came along, the household was a smooth sailing ship. There must have been adjustments when my mother started to work, but I was too young to remember. It's this family of mine that I am most grateful for in life. Without their love and support I'm not sure where I'd be today. The strong roots of faith, love, and family are what got me through the tough times and to the wonderful life I have today.

By the time I am about five years old, my sister Kathleen moves on with her life. She enters the convent. The day we drop her off and say goodbye, I am in shock. I can't imagine my life without her. I am very sad to say the least. In the following year my grandfather dies suddenly from a heart attack. Both my caretakers are quickly removed from my life, and I remember crying myself to sleep at night. I miss them terribly, and my whole world is different. It is a very sad time. This is when I receive my very first self-help lesson. I am in the first grade.

Frequently I visit my mother at the gift shop that my parents own. On one particular day my mother shows me two figurines. She explains to me in detail the meaning of each. There's the "Pessimist" and the "Optimist." She tells me I can choose only one. It is a rare occasion to take anything home from the gift shop, and I am so excited. I carefully think about which one I want and decide on the "Optimist." Looking back to that moment I realize that I made a conscious choice that day to be happy. Every morning I see the statue of the optimist on my dresser. As I get ready to start my day, I make the decision to be happy. I look to find all the things in my day to be happy about.

During that visit my mother told me there are always things in each and every day that can make me happy or sad. The "Pessimist" looks for the sad things or for what he is missing. The "Optimist" looks for the happy things and enjoys what he has. Even though they live in the same world, they see that world in different ways. I understood the message clearly then, even at my young age. It was very clever of my mother, and I learned that lesson well. Looking back now, I can see how that decision to be happy has defined my life. Thanks, mom.

Growing up in an Irish Catholic home I was taught about God early on. My mom used to tell me that even if I can't see what you are doing, God is always watching. I remember looking everywhere for that God. If my mom said it, I believed it. I searched and searched until one day I felt the presence within me. I became aware at a very young age that I am not alone.

In addition, prayer has always been a constant in my life, having been taught at a young age to pray. Very early on I just talked to God and received answers. The answers came in many forms. A feeling sometimes grabbed my attention followed by a thought. Sometimes I heard someone say something that resonated, even if the person was not speaking to me. Somehow though I always got answers and still do today.

I remember when I was in second or third grade my Catholic school went to the "Stations of the Cross." I became tearful when I realized the pain of Jesus. I had prior knowledge that Jesus died for our sins. I am sure I had been to the "Stations" before. I'd seen Him on the cross in church, but this was the first time I actually felt His pain. I realized the pain was real. I remember as if it were yesterday. I immediately told Jesus how sorry I was that He suffered. It's awful how His life was taken from Him. I gave Him my life right then and there in prayer. "You can have my life, I told Him with all the love in my heart."

Also, at about this same age I had an out of body experience. As children, we used to think it was fun to make ourselves pass out. We would get on our knees with someone behind us, and breathe in and out with deep breaths until we were dizzy. Then, as we held a breath, the person behind would wrap his arms around us and squeeze tight until we passed out.

Not the smartest thing to do but when I did it, I passed out. My spirit went out of my body, speeding across the earth like energy soaring. I was saying the whole time, "Here I am God! Here I am!" It felt as if I flew around the whole sphere in a flash, very close to the Earth. Then I slipped right back into my body and regained consciousness.

The point I am making by sharing this history with you is that throughout my entire life I have had a very strong connection to God, a friendly connection. When facing tough decisions I always asked for guidance. This doesn't mean I don't make plenty of mistakes along the way. Today I ask for guidance in everything I do. Then, I only asked when making the big decisions. Silly, I know but as Maya Angelou says, "When we know better, we do better."

My awareness and love of God has always been present in my consciousness. A saint or an angel I am not. As a matter of fact, my father told me once that I gave him more trouble than all my sisters put together! He said that in a loving way, of course. After all, I was daddy's little girl. But I did cause more than my share of trouble and heartache for my family, and for that I am not proud.

You are now invited to witness my journey from the horrors of hell to the heights of happiness. It doesn't happen overnight and it is not easy by any means, but with faith, prayer, a positive focus, discipline, and intelligent action, I succeed.

Fortune Cookie

Focus on the positive and you will see
Exactly how happy you are meant to be
Happiness is the ride, put it in stride
Then get moving and enjoy the ride

Destination's a must, for directions to go
Action with intention, enhance the show
Focus on the positive, be happy and free
With enough positives the negatives flee

"The Gift Gallery" Ambler, Pa. 1958 center: Terri age 5, Anne age 9

Success is to be measured not so much by the position one has reached in life, as by the obstacles he or she has overcome while trying to succeed.

- Booker T. Washington

Chapter II

The March into Hell

We all have different challenges in life and obstacles to overcome. The obvious question in your mind is probably, "How did someone with my background, from a loving family and a long standing friendship with God, end up living on welfare in a home for women?" It is understandable that you might ask this question. That very same question was in my mind at the time also.

At age seventeen my life is on track to fulfill my dream. The engagement to my high school sweetheart happens on graduation day. The only dream in my mind is to marry and have children. My fiancé Tom and I marry the following summer. We move into a small home in Ambler, Pa. Eleven months later our first son Jerome is born. Jerome is a family name on Tom's side. Eighteen months later our second son Danny enters the world. Dan is named after my father, Daniel Anthony. Soon after Danny is born, my husband and I separate. We are both young and overwhelmed at the time.

During our separation of about four months we attend marriage counseling, separately at first and then together. Before we are ready, at Tom's insistence we move back together; before long we file for divorce. Now our relationship turns ugly. My husband is in business with his mother and all properties, including our home and car, are in the business name. At the time of our divorce the business is barely getting by and the issue of money creates havoc. This period is by far the most chaotic of my life to that date.

Speaking with my own lawyer only upset the apple cart more. The settlement my husband and his mother offer me is a pittance, but seeking a realistic amount will destroy the business, and in the end my sons will have less. Coming from a solid family of love and faith, my prayer is for the best for my children. This is my priority. My sons deserve the best start in life that they can get.

Many crazy things happen before the answer to my prayer comes to me, but I won't go into the details now. Just know that I receive a clear answer; I decide not to sue the business. My lawyer cautions me that if I do not fight now for money and custody, I do not stand a chance to win at a future date. I understand and accept these consequences. The lawyer asks me what will happen if the boys' father decides to move in the future. I am certain that will not happen. Tom and his mother are locked into that business, for sure. Also, I know the answer to my prayer is a guided decision, and I have no doubts.

So Tom and I divorce without a fight from me. Walking away with a bit of furniture may appear to be stupid to many, but I am satisfied that my children will not be living on welfare. They will have all they need with plenty of love from all of us.

I sell my diamond engagement ring and a few other items to gather enough money for escrow on an apartment about ten miles away that I share with my friend Faith who is also going through a difficult period after the sudden death of her fiancé. I manage to buy a used car with $500.00 I receive from cashing in a life insurance policy.

A girlfriend's husband helps me find a 1969 Volkswagen Beetle that my children and I call Bugsy.

After the dust settles from the divorce, Tom and I share equal time with the boys: Monday, Wednesday and every other weekend with me, and every Tuesday, Thursday and every other weekend with Tom. It is not the dream I once had of family living, but for years this living arrangement works well.

I find work at a pharmacy located mid-way between my apartment and Tom's house. My sister, Eileen, knows the pharmacist and helps me get the job. My hours fit into my schedule with the boys so that babysitters are not needed. This is not an ideal life, by any means, but this lifestyle keeps both Tom and I connected with the boy's regular routine, and that is what is important to me.

After a year in the apartment, Faith decides to move out on her own. No longer able to afford the apartment, I decide to rent a house with my new boyfriend whom I intend to marry. This house provides more space and a yard for my sons; my life seems to be moving in a better direction.

Less than four years later a bomb explodes in my life. Tom and his mother sell the business; he moves hours away to Margate, NJ and takes the boys and his mother with him. The shock overwhelms me. I am living in a nightmare; only I can't wake up.

The boys move away, and I see them as often as I can, but with a failing car and not much money for travel, it is difficult. They are in second and fourth grades at the time. Being angry and resentful does not help my case, but this is how I feel. My relationship with the man I am living with also sours, and I move into the in-law suite of a friend's home temporarily.

With the help of my brother-in-law Jack I get a job with a pharmaceutical company that promises a bright future, once the position becomes permanent. To start, I am a part-time temp and am on call for any of three shifts daily. The promise is that after a certain period of time, I'd become a permanent employee with the best pay and benefits, along with the opportunity for further education.

This job gives me hope of building a better life for myself to share with my sons. For a few years I move back home with my parents. I buy a new car so I have a dependable means of transportation. As long as I have the hope of this job in my sight, I am able to cope. However, it isn't living, I am like a zombie with no emotions unless I am with my children; only then do I come alive. Outside of my time with them, I just do what I have to do. I look normal enough to others, but I am detached from any real emotion on the inside.

I can remember my father getting angry with me for not watching television and participating in family life. TV just brings up the emotions I am trying to keep in check. I do what I need to do, cook dinner, do dishes, and work when I am called. Outside of the must do's, I stay in my room writing and/or dancing. Writing is one exercise I do as a hobby, and dancing is something I have done since I was able to walk. I studied ballet and modern jazz all through grade school and a few years into high school. These activities help release my feelings. Going out dancing at night is the only real release that helps me escape my reality for a few hours. I just get lost in the music and dance.

The temp job gives me hope and keeps me going, that and, of course, seeing my sons. To get through each day I must visualize a better tomorrow. My present circumstances look nothing like the life plan of my younger days' vision. All I had ever wanted was to be a mom. I did realize my motherhood dream, but now it does not look the way I had imagined, outside of the love I feel for my two, amazing, young sons. We light up the room when we are together. One thing for sure is that we make every minute together count.

After a few years living with the false hope of changing my life for the better, another bomb explodes. The pharmaceutical job that gave me hope of a better future disappears, due to a company error. All the employees on the part-time temp waiting list are dismissed with no hope of a future call back. This news hits me hard. All my hope is gone.

My pain then becomes unbearable. It is difficult for me to get out of bed in the morning. I can't face the next several years feeling so hopelessly burdened. I just want to die. Suicide is not an option because I won't leave my sons with that memory. But death by other measures, in my mind at the time, is still acceptable. So I pray for God to take my life. I pray for death.

Believing that my prayer will be answered, I write a poem for my children, just some words of wisdom to live by. I begin cleaning out closets, organizing my writings, and things of that nature, fully expecting my life to be over soon. Every visit with my sons is even more meaningful to me since each visit may be the last time we are together.

During this waiting-for-death period an acquaintance helps me get a bartending job in a rock 'n roll bar in Philadelphia. It is a shot and beer joint that sailors frequent when docked at the Philly port. A live band plays for forty minutes every hour, and dancing girls with pasties and G-strings dance in between sets.

This job does not require my brain. All drinks are measured shots, and every drink is the same price. All I need is to show up, smile and be friendly to the customers. Looking like the happiest person in the world, I wait for death. Only a few people there know of my sadness.

Every night is a rock 'n roll fantasy for me. I assume a role and act it out all evening. Many nights I include some of the regular customers in my fantasy. This role playing helps me stay out of touch with reality, while entertaining the customers at the same time. Along with acting out a story line my body moves to every musical beat. Dancing is in my blood.

My life continues in this mode for months, just waiting for death, living without care for my present or future life. The only time I touch ground emotionally is with my sons. There is no goal or focus in my sight. During this period I lose further touch with reality by using drugs and alcohol. I have used prescription diet pills for a long time, especially when I was on call for three shifts at the pharmaceutical company. The pills help keep me awake with the added benefit of numbing my feelings. At this time I also take meth, a street drug usually stronger than diet pills and better able to numb my feelings. The only time I come into reality is with my children. That is the only reality I can handle, being with them.

As the months go by, after a visit with my sons it becomes harder and harder to get back to my fantasy realm. To look at me, I appear to be the happiest, most fun person in the world, dancing and smiling, talking and making up wild stories to keep the customers entertained. The girls dancing in between sets complain to the owners because I am making bigger tips than they; eventually, I am allowed to dance only when the band plays.

Finally, after many months I receive the answer to my prayer for death- *no death for me*. At this point I am crushed. I am in shock. My life is unbearable. I have no direction and no idea how to get out of the rut I am in. I remember crying and crying to God in disbelief, feeling hopeless. Breathing becomes difficult. As I gasp for air in between sobs, I remember being angry with God and feeling mislead by His direction. "You need to help me!" I remember crying. "I am lost." I also remember praying to St. Anthony, the saint that is known to help find lost objects. I know for certain that I am lost.

Without strength, having no hope, and no thought of how to manage change, I surrender my life to God once again, and I write this prayer for strength.

Prayer for Strength

Please give me strength Lord
I know only you can
To live not for the world of today
But for the Kingdom of Yours

Help me Lord to do Your will
For I know at times I am weak
Teach me Lord Your way
Because with You I wish to stay

Thank You Lord
I know You are here
As often as I let You down
For me You are always around

I feel Your presence
Only You do I trust
I give You my life
Before I return to dust

Take me Lord
Make me worthy
I am what I am
But with You I know I can

Without the hope of death as an escape, where can I go from here? Being lost in a world that does not resemble the life I once knew, I drift through the motions of the life I now have. There is so much to tell, but in this short overview the main fact to know is at this time my reality is a living horror to me. This nightmare seems unending, with no way out.

Then God pulled the rug out from under me. Many obstacles cross my path intensifying my anger. One major issue is the fact I did not get to spend the previous summer with my boys, as was verbally agreed. This anger built up in me because I was off from work that summer with nothing but time to share with my children. Having been denied the summertime by their father, I sought the advice of a lawyer that has jurisdiction in both Pennsylvania and New Jersey. His advice is to kidnap the boys, *his term exactly*, because then I'd have more power in court. This advice sounds absurd to me, and I go to the family priest for advice. All the priest can offer me at the time is prayer, which I gratefully accept, but it gives me no visible, immediate help. My parents have no advice for me either. No one has any answers, so my anger just simmers all through the winter months.

My frustration over the past summer's issue remains in my consciousness. In March, I call the boys' father and demand I get my summer time with them, or I will proceed with a lawyer. He tells me that I can have them for the month of June, take it or leave it. His answer would not be so bad had they not been in school that year until June 16th or 17th. My ire rises, and the simmer begins to boil.

My car, the lifeline to my children, presents another obstacle. It is only a few years old but has over 50,000 miles due to all the many back and forth trips to visit Jerome and Danny. After I spend thousands of dollars to repair the transmission, mostly all the money I have, not to mention the lack of use for a week, the car still does not shift properly. That week my father tells me that the TV show 20/20 reported that this national transmission company rips off the public with bad service. This information just adds fuel to my anger.

While working through these obstacles, I continue to bartend. In May of 1986, the job I had lost with the pharmaceutical company reappears, not with any chance of permanence, but for a temporary two to four weeks. A popular drug this company produces has been pulled off the shelves for public safety reasons, and the company needs a crew around the clock to get the product back on the shelves across the country, as quickly as possible.

The part-time temps are all called to work, and we work seven days straight, two weeks in a row. I have no time to get to the doctor for any diet pills, and no time to purchase drugs on the street. In addition, my car's transmission is in for repair at another shop so I have to rent a car. Without my emotional dampener of diet pills or meth for two weeks, no dance to release my pain, my feelings of anger rise to the surface fast. With each passing day my emotions just grow stronger.

This job offers no fantasy escape, and the anger that is brewing from the past months keeps expanding. My reality becomes clear, and it feels as if I am playing a part in a movie, but I did not receive the script. Nothing seems real to me. I imagine it is the same feeling that one might experience with amnesia. People obviously know me, but I do not recognize my life. I am living a nightmare.

The pain of missing my children, the anger over the situation of not spending the summer with them, the car issues, having no drugs to help numb the pain, not being able to dance it out, and to top it all, being called back to this fabulous job without the hope it once promised, becomes too much for me to bear. I see clearly how these issues combine to push me over my limit. It is impossible for me to escape reality now. Looking back, I see the brilliance in every little detail, definitely a divinely guided plan.

Pay day comes on the second Friday of work, which happens to be the start of Memorial Day weekend. The pay we receive is for two full seven day weeks. Seeing the amount on my paycheck is the last straw for me, it pushes something in me I have never experienced before or after this day. Something in me snaps. My mind uncoils like a popped spring, and the motion releases pent up pressure inside my brain. I totally disconnect. My emotions become dead, detached, and I feel nothing. Without any thought of what is next, I walk to my locker, take my belongings, and proceed out the door. I walk out just when I am scheduled to start the next shift.

I see myself do and say things as in a movie, but I'm not really being present. If someone asks me a question, I say the first thing that enters my mind, whether it makes sense or not. Looking back, I see myself calling out for help, but no one really knows I am in trouble.

Now I have the money I need to take my children on a fun vacation. That is all I want to do; spend some time having fun with my boys. I just need something to fix this hell I am in. I know only a miracle can fix my life, and I believe that a miracle is imminent. God brought me here, and God will fix it.

At home I pack my rental car and head for Jerome and Danny's house at the Jersey shore. Because of the holiday weekend the roads are teaming with cars, and the drive takes over five hours. By the time I arrive, the boys are not home. Not being able to see them really puts me over the edge. I recall calling my sister Eileen to ask her if she knows where the boys are. Again, this I see now as a call for help, because in my right mind I would never ask her that question. She is not in touch with my sons that way.

In hindsight I had been calling for help for months prior to this incident because I did not know how to get out of the hole I was in. My parents knew I was not right, but they did not know what to do. To the people I worked with at the bar, I was in much better shape than they were, or at least I appeared to be from their point of view. So my life just kept spiraling out of control.

As the weekend continues, my state of mind keeps unraveling. I spend most of the time driving the rental car aimlessly, not knowing where to go without my sons. The rest of the time I am with people who know nothing about me, and there is no one to save me. When I get tired of driving, I rent a limo at the casino to drive me around to look for my boys. The whole weekend passes with crazy acts, hunting for my children. By the time the weekend is over, my money is gone from hotel rooms, limo rides, and God only knows what else. God knew exactly what He was doing.

On Tuesday morning, I pull up to my sons' house about seven-thirty in the morning. To see my sons is all I can think about. From the bedroom window they see me, and they come running out as excited as ever. "Look at mom's new car!" they were saying. "Come on and take a ride" I call out. Running to me, with no shirts and without shoes, the boys jump in my car. As I begin to drive, we are all so excited to be together. For an instant, it is pure joy.

After a mile or so of driving my son Jerome says, "We should go back to get ready for school." Danny says, "Can't we go for just a little longer?" Something in the way Danny spoke penetrates my emotional void, and I began driving further away. Without a plan or concern for consequence, I tell the boys, "Everything is OK. We don't have to go back. We are on an adventure." I fill their heads with one of my fantasies, with no clue as what to do next.

First we stop to get them some clothes to wear. They pick out some shirts to put on, and Danny picks a shirt that reads, "No Problem" in large letters. I make up the story I have a job in Disney World, and we are going there for the summer. I buy them all sorts of clothes for the trip. Having no money left from my spree, I simply write a bad check, knowing there is not enough in my account to cover the expense. Exiting the store we are elated and having fun living this fantasy. From here we continue shopping in many stores, writing more bad checks. My mind gives no thought as to what is next, and I have no sense of fear or any kind of sensation to warn me to stop. I only see the joy of being with my sons.

My experience that day is hard to describe. In the moment, I am elated watching the events unfold and seeing the joy on Jerome and

Danny's faces. The key word here is: watch. That is the best way to describe me that day, I watch every little detail. There is no thought in my mind prior to any action. I had not planned to take the boys that morning. I just wanted to see them. Now I view my actions that day as an elaborate call for help. I am so lost and do not know how to get back to my life. For many months my plan had been death. My calls for help over the past months went unnoticed. It is a blessing that I had no money by the time I saw the boys because only God knows where I might have landed with them.

Our adventure is all fun and games until I stop to see a friend late in the afternoon. My friend Lyn is at work, but her husband, Alan, is there. Alan sees immediately that I am not right. He quizzes me why I have the boys on a school day. It is clear to me that he is not on my side, and I begin to make a fast exit. As the boys and I start for the door, Alan grabs a hold of Danny. He tries to get to Jerome, but cannot reach. It is a real scene, and Jerome and I finally make a break, but Danny is left behind. The tide turns, and the fun stops. There is no fantasy in my mind that can be fun without both my boys present.

After driving for hours Jerome and I stop in a mall parking lot, and we sleep in the car. I don't know where to go. In the morning, I decide to go to my sister Anne's house in Delaware. Jerome and I are both hungry, and I am out of resources. We arrive just as the family is walking out the door to go to work and school. To my surprise she knows nothing of my adventure. She gives us a warm welcome and lets us in, as she departs. Jerome has something to eat, and we both fall asleep only to awaken to the police at the front door. The officer puts me in handcuffs, and another officer takes Jerome away.

Upon my arrival at police headquarters, I am questioned to see if I am coherent and/or dangerous. Then I sit and wait, still in handcuffs, for the decision. Hours pass before the handcuffs are finally removed, and I am escorted to a place out in the woods that has cots lined along the wall like an army barracks. The next day I am transported to Atlantic County Jail Facility in Mays Landing, New Jersey. I remain in jail for two weeks because my family does not want to bail me out until they decide the best course of action to help me.

My cell mates call me the 'crazy white girl' because first, I am the only white person there, and second, I dance about the place in an effort to stay upbeat. Jail is a horrible place to be. I reach the nadir when my mother visits me, and I communicate with her by phone while sitting across from her, separated by glass. So much shame I feel in that moment.

The jail facility let me out on my own after two weeks. Once home, my family has an intervention. My sisters want me to go for drug treatment, a thirty day program. At first I put up a fight. I know my problem is not the drugs. I haven't used drugs in almost a month at this point, and I've never used needles. My sisters do not know much about drugs, and I remember telling them I just need a vacation with Jerome and Danny. But the more excuses I give to fight the treatment center, the more clearly I see how I sound just like a drug addict. I know I am not able to change their minds that my problems are not caused by drugs, so I agree to go for treatment. How bad can rehab be? My sister Eileen promises to bring the boys to visit when I go for treatment.

My date to go away is a few weeks away. My friend Lyn is a nurse and understands treatment. She knows me well and tells me that when I get to the clinic I will be asked to choose either the drug treatment facility or the mental treatment. Lyn explains that the doctors are the same, and many of the treatments are the same; however, the drug facility has many more activities and the time will pass faster. So, when asked that question, I choose the drug treatment facility. Once there, I am actually excited to discover the treatment includes family therapy. My heart and mind at the time still have hope of a miracle to fix my life.

The treatment center is actually a good experience for me. I learn many skills and am happy because I believe that when the counselors hear my story, they will help me fix my life with some magical solution. I never wanted to do the drugs, a lesson I learned in high school, but I did not know any other way to cope with the emotional hell I was living separated from my children. Here at the clinic I see so many people struggling with many different issues. My roommate is an alcoholic who had been sexually abused by her minister father. She must prepare for a family therapy session where she intends to confront him and out him to her mother, a very intense drama. Another woman cannot stop drinking and is in treatment for her fourth time. A gentleman in our group is discovered to be suicidal in an art therapy class, and has a breakdown. Every day brings a new, real case to light.

Many people in the treatment center have spiritual awakenings during my stay. This is interesting to watch. I witness a few people have real personality changes when they wake up to a power greater than themselves. This is a beautiful experience for me to see. Unfortunately, I do relate to many people there. I connect with a few but do not have the struggle of withdrawal, or the pangs of anxiety to get high. My struggle is sadness. I am just so, so sad.

One group exercise stands-out in my memory. My first weekend at the center is the July 4th weekend, and this exercise is for fun to help the twenty men and women in my group get to know one another. We all are asked to choose a famous person we look up to and explain why. When my turn arrives, I pick Madonna because I believe singing and dancing are fun and exciting, and to be able to bring happiness and joy to others this way seems awesome to me. Remember, at the time dancing is an emotional outlet for me. Who am I kidding…it still is. Anyway, I take criticism from a few group members for my choice. Most of the group members chose heroic icons.

The next morning at breakfast, one group member places the newspaper in front of me with a headline that reads, "What's Wrong with Idolizing Madonna?" The article goes on to speak of Madonna's empire, and how well she markets herself. Seeing the timeliness of this headline gives me a good feeling, because I see this as a Godsend to remind me, I am not alone.

When my thirty days in rehab are over, I am asked to go to a long-term treatment facility, a home for women, a women's half-way house that provides additional treatment and then helps women transition to a productive life. So far I've said I am a drug addict and an alcoholic to stay in the drug facility. I am not moving forward this way. I am angry and confused. I go to this home with no intention to stay. I have some money stashed, not much, fifty dollars or so, but enough for a bus or train ride out of town. I pray for direction where to go.

In the meantime, while I wait for God's direction, I abide by the house rules. The first order of business is a one-on-one meeting with each resident. First is Jeannie. She is the senior resident, and is very understanding of my resistance to be here. We go outside and sit in the shade of a giant tree. As I tell her my story she cries, and informs me that even if I am not an addict, I will benefit from the service provided. She explains that the therapy is very helpful, and the guidance from the counselors will help me find a suitable job. After speaking with Jeannie, I feel a bit better, but still have no intention to stay. Each day I look for a sign of where to go. Finally, after a week of silence from my inner source, I become enlightened to the fact: I am in the right place.

As the one-on-ones continue with the rest of the women, the counselors get wind that I am denying to be an addict. I get pulled into the office and they insist that if I want to stay in this house I will admit I am an addict. They confront me with the fact that I admitted to my own addiction in the treatment facility, and had

I not been an addict I would never have done that. Now my head spins once again because my denial only makes me look more like an addict. My explanation only falls on deaf ears. I try to explain my situation. I now know that I am in the right place. I know I need help to get on a life path. So I just continue to act the part. The whole misunderstanding just adds to the bizarre nightmare that is now my life. I move forward as an addict.

At this point I wish that drugs were the cause of my problem because by removing the drugs, my life would get better. This is not the case for me. Removing the drugs and alcohol is easy for me; living and facing the pain of my life is not. Nothing will make living my life easy for me. So I make a promise to not use drugs and alcohol for at least five years and then access where I am in life. I go to AA meetings with the group and listen to all the struggles that recovering people deal with. I do not relate to these struggles, and I count my blessings.

The reality that there is no magical cure for my life hits me, and the darkness of the truth overtakes my consciousness. The only way out of this hell is to put one foot in front of the other and walk through the pain. Finally, with the acceptance of my reality, I can begin to heal. I live in this home where no one is my friend. Chores are divided and rotated. Some meals are tolerable. Other meals are awful, depending on the rotation of cooks.

While living in this home, I listen and learn all I can. I finally realize that I must have made some really bad choices to end up here needing so much help. Every other resident has a sordid past that brought them here; I am from a great background, and my guilt for being here overwhelms me. In fear, I ask God to help me make the choices in life that bring me closer to Him.

As my time passes in this house, women come and go. As one woman leaves, another enters. Some do really well, but sadly, others do not. Two of the women that leave the house only weeks before I do, die within the year; both of these women were in the house only as an alternative to jail. Change needs to come from within, and unfortunately these women did what they needed to do on the outside to get through their time there, but they were not open to change. God bless.

The rule of the house before one takes a job is a minimum of five interviews, and the job accepted must allow the residents to be back to the house by 6:00 pm. During the adjustment period on the job the home for women offers continued support.

The interview process is a great learning experience for me. I interview with a local bank, a high-end lighting company, a salon, a local office, and a car dealer. The car dealer hours are not acceptable but will count as an interview. The job I am counting on is the lighting company. During the first three job interviews I am honest about where I am living and the circumstances of my life. However, the truth does not help me. I am turned away from the lighting company because the manager feels I will not able to handle the stress of the position due to my circumstances. I do have an offer from the bank position, but the pay is not sufficient to support me.

Next I interview for the salon and a car dealer; I omit the facts of my circumstances and leave a gap on my resume. Surprisingly, no one asks about the missing time. I receive an offer from both interviews. The car dealership really grabs my attention with the potential to earn $25,000.00 the first year.

Back at the house, I present the situation to my counselors. They give me the run down on the rules and tell me I am free to leave the house at any time. There is never a lock on the door. Or, they suggest that I take a different job for my transition, and then accept the job at the dealership in a month or so. My disappointment is obvious, but I accept the rules. I do not choose to leave now and walk out without the support of my therapists. Immediately, I begin to look at the want ads to see what other position may suit me. I circle a few ads and intend to follow up on them tomorrow.

The next morning as the daily routine sets in, I am called into the office. Both counselors are in the office, along with the house manager. They ask how I am. I tell them I am fine and am looking for a suitable job, and that I have a few leads to follow up. The house manager tells me how they are all shocked, and pleased at the same time, by the way I accepted the news of not being able to take the job offer from the car dealership. I let them know I am disappointed, but that I understand the rules. I express my appreciation to all of them for their help over the past months, and explain my intention to leave the house with their blessing and support. I will follow the rules.

After all is said, they give me their blessing to take the job at the car dealership. Because I had not given them an argument and had accepted their decision, they bend the rules. They all feel that this job at the dealership offers me a good opportunity, and they are willing to support me in this venture. I am just thrilled. My counselors lay out a few new rules for me to follow, with a new curfew time to match my work schedule, and a few make-up chores for the ones I will miss. All seems fair to me. I have the support of the group, and this is enough for me.

Now I begin my new life. I start from scratch, with only a plan to survive. Fear of failure lives within, with no understanding of how I landed here, and my only wish is to make good choices each and every day. My prayer for strength continues because I know I cannot get through this challenge on my own. I retain all the information my therapists taught me, and recognize the Godsend this house turned out to be. Even though I did not enjoy one minute being in this house, I understand the valuable tools given me, and intend to use each and every one.

Here is where my fight to be happy begins. I must choose to be happy or allow the sadness to consume me. Death is not an option, so I must keep my mind focused on the positive. What we look for in life affects what we see, and I look for the good that each day holds. I do not focus on what is missing: my sons and the life I once had with them. If I allow myself to focus on missing my sons, I will not survive; this I know for sure. So please, come along with me and see just how I manage to succeed in this new life.

Broken Wings

With broken wings
My new life begins
Becoming aware
That life is not fair

Starting over again
My broken heart on mend
With hope in mind
Recalls, love is kind

The sadness surrounds me
But an optimist I must be
For every choice is mine
And my life is on the line

A broken spirit without wings
A task too difficult to begin
Strength, delivered from above
Shows as borrowed wings from the Dove

Terri's Wedding Day July 15, 1972

Sensitivity awakes, feelings to explore
Sadness lingers from years before
Inner strength comes, strong to the core
A new life is waiting, outside my door

Chapter III

Borrowed Wings

The story of my success begins with the question, "How am I to be happy in the midst of hell?" Achieving happiness seems hopeless to me at the time, but I have made a commitment to live. But how do I survive when every circumstance of my life looks and feels so wrong?

The puzzle pieces of my life don't fit, but somehow they are locked in place. With every dream of mine shattered and gone forever, how is it possible for me to be happy? Nothing can change the past; nothing will fix it. My life is no longer familiar. To hate every part of my surroundings will not get me through. So what can I do?

I pray. My prayer for strength is a constant in my Life. I now wonder if that prayer actually made my life more difficult. To gain strength, one gets more and more difficult tasks to overcome, much as a body-builder lifts heavier and heavier weights to gain the strength needed to succeed. Today my prayer is much simpler: "Thank You for Your strength, Lord, thank You for Your power."

The feeling of the 'sadness' within me best compares to the 'sadness' in the movie "The Never Ending Story." The hero of the story has to pass through the 'sadness' that is like a thick jungle of all sadness condensed. It pulls on the hero like quicksand. The hero and his horse have to keep moving or be consumed in the depths of the 'sadness.' The hero knows the 'sadness' will pass once he makes his way out of the jungle, but it is so difficult to fight his way through. The hero is totally surrounded by 'sadness.' Then his horse, his trusted companion, dies in the 'sadness.' Now the hero really has to force himself to fight the 'sadness' to move on.

My feelings are exactly like the hero in the story. I have to fight the sadness every day to get through this time in my life. The fight is a constant energy pull. There will be an end to the sadness one day in the future, and there is no other choice for me but to choose happiness or be consumed in sadness. I learn to play games with my mind to keep my thoughts occupied from wandering into the dark trenches of the sadness. A positive focus is what helps me get through many days.

By learning the hard way, I know how imperative it is to keep my mind busy, or down the slippery slope of sadness my thoughts will carry me. If my mind goes to thoughts of my sons, wondering what they are doing, how are they feeling, are they happy, these thoughts only take me to a deep, dark place where survival is impossible. With persistence, over time I learn to just say, "STOP! that thought," and pay attention to what is right here now. Mind control is a must for me. In weak moments, saying continuous prayers works to keep my thoughts from wandering off. Always at night, going to sleep, I repeat prayer after silent prayer to hold my mind's attention.

I am not able to keep photos of the boys around. I carry some in my wallet but do not have any on my desk at work or at home. This, in and of itself, is a strange occurrence for me because I love to have photos all around me as reminders of my loved ones and our times shared. But during this period of my life, photo reminders are a detriment to my survival.

The saying, "What doesn't kill you makes you stronger" comes to mind, and I am gaining strength. I find the constant pain in my heart hard to live with. Faith in God is the only answer that comes to me as to how I make it through this time. For sure, God carries me through because I do not have the strength.

In my younger years when I was separated from my sister Kathleen, who was like a mother to me, I often wonder if that was God's way of preparing me for my life separated from my sons. I believe it was. Eventually I find the strength I need. Is it possible that my own prayer had created a more difficult path for me? Perhaps, but gratitude still takes over my heart because this path brings me to the miracle I am living today. I make another mistake with prayer, if a mistake can actually be made with prayer. When I begin my new career, I pray for confidence. Once again, I gain confidence by attracting all sorts of people and circumstances that knock me down repeatedly. Just the nature of sales provides enough rejection without several people in my life knocking me down over and over again. Finally, my confidence kicks-in and I say, "STOP, enough already!"

So my new life has begun, but I am broken and not able to walk through the pain alone. Nothing in my life feels good to me, NOTHING! All I can do is put one foot in front of the other. I have no other choice. This is my life, like it or not. I struggle to keep a positive focus in order to move forward, in order to survive. Only with faith, and help from above, is moving forward possible. I must guard my thoughts constantly to keep from falling into that dark abyss of sadness.

My new job in the auto business starts January 5, 1987. It is a cold, wintery day in Pennsylvania, and the opening day of a Volkswagen Center under new management and the owner also owns a Chrysler-Plymouth-Dodge center across the street. Both store managers, after my interviews, wanted me to work in their store, so they agree to split my time. My schedule has me in each store on different days. This surprise is both flattering and overwhelming at the same time. I am nervous about all the product knowledge required, along with the added co-workers to get to know.

The advantage of working in both stores is that the added workload keeps my mind busy. It also offers a better opportunity for me to earn more money. (Those precious Wing's from above, God's saving grace!) Soon I realize that no other sales person is assigned shifts in both stores. As overwhelming as learning all the products seems to be, my gratitude takes over and I see this opportunity as a blessing for keeping my mind occupied. In addition, I see my own value. There were six new hires for the VW grand opening, and I am the only one chosen to work in both stores.

My placement in both stores is not common, and I wonder why the other sales people don't object. This advantage teaches me early in my career that the demographics for the different products vary. The clients for these brands are as different as night and day. Looking back, I see clearly how this learning experience prepped me for my life ahead, to be able to make changes in the future more easily, without fear. I witness so many people stuck in a rut and afraid to move on to another product.

As time passes, the reason there is no jealousy becomes clear to me; the other salespeople don't want to put in the effort to learn both products. These sales people are 'comfortable' with the brand they know and are stuck in their comfort zone. This attitude seems absurd to me, but I do not complain because I am called to whichever store is busiest, regardless of where I am scheduled. The more people I speak with, the better opportunity I have to sell a car. I count my blessings.

Total awareness of my thoughts is a must at all times. To know what my mind is thinking is a matter of survival for me. Prayer, faith, and constantly choosing good thoughts carry me through this time. The first month is a challenge, and I am very grateful to have the support of my counselors to help manage my transition. I tell no one at work where I live. The first month passes quickly, and my time to move out on my own arrives. Actually, I am to share an apartment with a woman who moved out of the home for women a few weeks prior to me.

My first grocery shopping trip is stamped in my memory forever. As I reach for the food stamps in the grocery check-out line, I feel humiliated. My mind races and flashes thoughts of how is this *MY* life? How is this possible? My thoughts continue to race… I worked from the age of thirteen, even younger if you count babysitting and helping my mother in the gift shop. Fear and panic take hold as I remember the thousands of dollars I had given to my fiancé before we were married to pay the taxes for the business. How does my life now look like this? How? These thoughts just keep rotating around and around in my mind. I get dizzy and feel faint. Why am I here? What is ahead for me? My panic begins to expand as my head and heart throb. This panic attack is a first for me, and I haven't a clue what I should do.

I feel nauseous, and I begin to shake as I hand the food stamps to the cashier; all the while I promise myself never to be in this position again. My mind still whirls as I slowly walk out of the store, and my surroundings became a bit hazy. The experience is surreal. I put one foot in front of the other as I hold the cart tightly, and I keep walking while trying to breathe deep to keep myself from passing out. I do not understand why this rush of emotion overtakes me. Still dizzy, I head back to my apartment. When I arrive, the front door is unlocked and ajar, but my roommate is not there. The open door only adds to the eeriness of my day's experience. Two days later, my roommate still cannot be found, and my counselors find me a new roommate. My original roommate, sadly, does not survive the year. She went right back into an active addiction, and I never heard from her again. Her mother came to pick up her few belongings.

My new roommate is a woman who is also separated from her children. She too, just started a new job. There is a comfort in knowing we understand each other's pain. We both have very different stories but the same outcome. Yet, at the same time, the reality of living with a stranger haunts me. We'd met at the home, but circumstances just threw us together; we are not friends, at least not yet.

The place we share is an old, large house converted into three apartments. We live on the first floor. The house has a large covered porch on two sides, and the property has many large, old trees. This house could be a beautiful place with a lot of attention, but unfortunately it is not. The house is worn, drafty, and just plain battered from years of neglect, but this house is our home for now.

Here again my family comes to my rescue. My apartment gets furnished with bits and pieces from all of my sisters' homes. A few of my sisters and their husbands show up the day I move in with a truck and unload. They cover everything down to a napkin holder. Did I mention that my family is my biggest blessing? My family's generosity overwhelms me, and renders me speechless. Together, my roommate and I have had nothing but some bedroom furniture. We had planned to use paper plates with plastic utensils. Can it be possible to be so grateful, and yet still feel sick inside at the same time?

To be in such a needy position, demanding such help from my family makes me feel horrible. My sisters all have young families to take care of and here they are taking care of me. On the positive side, the kindness my sisters show gives me a sense of urgency to make this new life of mine work, no matter what.

I look around and see the reality of just how awful the circumstances of my life are. I see nothing around me that is mine. Everything in the apartment is mix-matched with nothing chosen because I love it. This fact creates a sinking feeling in me. My wardrobe is only a few pieces of clothing purchased with $100.00 given to me by my father because none of my old cloths are appropriate for business. That is my entire closet. One saving grace is the piggy-back washer/dryer that comes with the apartment. Thank God for the small luxuries in life.

A feeling of disgust comes over me every time I walk in the apartment door. This feeling is not a help to my survival, and I need to change how I feel. I recognize the need to change my feelings, but how? How can I change this feeling when what I feel is the truth? The way I feel is real. With no clue how to stop feeling bad about my environment, I pray for help. Prayer is my answer to everything, and still is.

It takes a few months until my prayer is answered, although the time seems much longer. One night as I sit at the kitchen table, a thought of my sister Anne and her family comes to mind. This was their table for many years, and the thought of happy, family meals filter into my consciousness. The love I imagine shared at this table changes the way I see the room, and my feelings begin to shift. I start to look around at the rest of the apartment, and I notice the sofa from Rosemary's home, a chair from Eileen, a table from Kathleen, and I begin to see the love from all my sister's families gathered here. My heart begins to warm, and I start to feel better about my surroundings.

In a flash, the realization hit me that my prayer is now answered. My apartment is still the same apartment, nothing changed except the way I perceive the images in my mind. I sit in silence and just look around the living room stunned, in awe. This change in me feels like a miracle. I sit and breathe with relief. I now begin to believe this new life may work. This moment is my first feeling of real peace in many years. Thank God. These new perceptions create new feelings within me about my surroundings and my life. And so the saying goes: Change your thoughts and you change your world. My whole apartment is transformed, and yet nothing changed but my own interpretation.

Many more months pass, and waking in the morning still remains difficult. The first moment of consciousness hits me with the reality of my situation; the nightmare is true. I pray first for my children, and then for the strength needed to get out of bed. My mental training kicks in. I need to keep my mind busy, so I play silly games. Some days I time myself to see how long it takes to get ready, not beating the clock, just watching and being aware of every minute, being curious of every little detail, sort of like narrating each step to an unseen audience.

On many days I choose a word to see how many times I can use the word during the day. Other times I just make a list in my mind of all things blue, or red, etc. Anything to keep my mind occupied, just as you might do with a two year old child on a road trip. The word games seem to be more fun and work better on a prolonged scale. I pick easy, everyday words that can be worked into normal conversations. The most entertaining words I recall are hilarious, fabulous, juicy and the one which provided the most fun- the word 'really.'

'Really' can be used in so many ways and also in multiples, "I am really, really, really, really, r-e-a-l-l-y...hungry." I have so much fun using this word that I use it several days in a row, each time trying to beat the previous day's record. "Really? Really! "Did I r-e-a-l-l-y do that?" "Really, tell me more!" "That is so really not going to happen." I think you get the point. The funniest thing is that after several days of saying 'really' in so many ways, by the time I move on to another word, other employees have adopted the word 'really' and begin using it. This fact is simply hysterical! Games like this help keep my mind busy and actually make me smile.

Several more months pass, and I become better at keeping focused on what is in front of me. The sadness still is a challenge, but with every passing day my gratitude increases because I feel God's power and strength helping me through each day. I pray in thanksgiving every night that one more day is passed.

Time keeps moving on, and the circumstances of my life do not change, but somehow I am able to adapt. By accepting the fact that this is my life now, and by making the most of what I have, my optimistic outlook kicks in to help. My famous words among my friends at the time are, "Oh, well!" which is my way of saying: Accept what you can't change.

My main focus is to find something in front of me to be happy and grateful for. Every time a customer walks in, my gratitude kicks in, and I do my best to focus on the task at hand, selling a car. Shoppers usually keep me busy for hours at a time. When there are no customers, I take a walk outside and appreciate the beauty of nature. Trees are especially powerful in helping me feel peace, and fortunately Pennsylvania is abundant with trees. Flowers in the warm months also bring me good feelings. I love flowers.

Feeling good is imperative for getting me through the day in peace. The sadness is always there, but learning to think about things that bring me happiness helps make my life easier under these circumstances. The more I focus on happiness, the more I find to be happy about.

My days off, when I get to spend time with my sons, is the true joy that I live for. Nothing compares to our time together, even to this day. All of us just light up inside when we see each other and our love can be seen by any bystander. The love we share is understood. The harsh circumstances of my life vanish when the three of us are together. Our visits are precious to all of us. We share many activities. I have become more of a friend than a parent. Looking back, I see many advantages that have developed due to our separation, but at the time, I can see no benefit.

Leaving my sons after our time together always pulls my heartstrings. Once again, I need to change my thoughts about the situation. This is much more difficult than the apartment situation due to the emotions attached, so I pray for help to see the positive. My head already knows the answer. My sons are living a better life than I am able to provide them at the time. Mentally, I can see the benefit for them, but my emotions are too difficult to handle. My tears are the outlet for the negative energy that fills me upon departing, and luckily, I have a long ride home to allow my tears to flow.

Once home, I need to pull myself together and focus on something positive. Much discipline is required on my part, but I focus with determination. I know the consequence of not being positive, and I am committed to make this life of mine work, no matter what! By living with my pain, but choosing to be happy, I discover the answer to the question that was asked at the beginning of this chapter: Is it possible to be happy in the middle of hell? Only if you choose to be; Happiness is a choice, your choice.

Pain does not have to mean the absence of happiness. Pain is oftentimes a reminder that we need to change ourselves in some way. The uncomfortable feelings we have can act as a catalyst for us to move in another direction, a push from the universe, if you can imagine that. In life our resistance actually causes pain. Acceptance of pain will eliminate the suffering. When in pain, awareness of our resistance is not always easy to see, but the truth lies in the pain. Change what you can, accept what you cannot change.

My living situation at the time is unchangeable. My circumstances are very painful for me, but once I accept the fact that this is my life, and end resistance, I am able to change my focus, and in turn create a better life. The pain is still there, but by deciding to be happy, no matter what, I shift into happiness; A kind of harmony, in the midst of change.

My work days are long. The General Manager at the dealership is one of those people put in my life to boost my confidence. All he does is try to knock everyone down. To me he appears to believe that his job is to belittle all beneath him, and everyone at the dealership is beneath him, in his opinion. The foul language he uses, I will not attempt to repeat here, but know that his language is not acceptable in any format.

Whenever I need to set an appointment for a customer to come in, I make sure it is not on the GM's watch. To avoid contact is my best defense. When avoidance is not an option, I learn very quickly to bring him the first sale's order incomplete. That way when he rejects the order, all I need to do is complete the form, because whatever is presented him the first time, is rejected. So with an incomplete form, I do less work. Seems crazy, but that is the best way to work with this man.

There is a gentleman by the name of Frank that works in the Chrysler store. He is an expert at selling and is very busy all the time. A few of the salesmen there tell me not to bother speaking with him because Frank doesn't talk to any new employees until they are working in the store for more than a year; "Too much turnover for me to waste precious time," he says. He is a funny man, and he takes me under his wing almost immediately. The other employees are shocked. Frank is the one who teaches me how to outsmart the GM with the incomplete sales form on the first approach. I feel blessed to have Frank on my side. Friends on the job there are plentiful. I love the people I work with, and I learn plenty in this first year. Work is the only place where I almost feel normal. I learn the ropes quickly, and my confidence builds with every passing month.

Work consumes my life for the most part, but still leaves too much down time for my mind to wonder. For many years I've written poems and stories to pass time; however, during this period I need a more directed focus. I see an ad in a magazine for a writing course. The course is designed to teach how to write children's books. The assignments come in the mail and allow a certain period of time for completion. Then the work is mailed back for critique. This writing course by mail is a much slower process than today's internet, but the writing assignments are one more activity to add to my mental process during this sad period.

To keep myself busy is the plan. As long as I am busy, I am OK. When not visiting my sons on my day off, I visit my parents who live about forty minutes away. My parents are up in years, and mom is failing a bit, due to a few strokes. I do whatever I can to help them with errands, and we usually go out to lunch. To visit with them is always a comfort. So many happy memories stem from this loving home where I grew up and the parents who have given me so much.

As the final quarter of the year rolls in, my pay stubs are not even close to the $25,000.00 that had been advertised. I am barely making ends meet even with sharing half the expenses. "How will I ever have a place of my own?" I wonder. Most months I sell as many cars as the top salesmen, but the money is just not there. I begin to question what I can do to make more money. I do like the work here, and I love the people, but I intend to live a better life. Some of the salesmen in the Chrysler store are paid a higher base pay than others, and I feel my value is par with theirs. I ask my boss for more money, and he tells me to sell more cars. I am not happy with that answer, but do not see any other options at this time.

A Godsend comes to me now in a very unusual way. My car insurance is coming due and I need $600.00. The time keeps getting closer and closer, and I don't see the money I need come in. I'm not able to ask my family. I need to stand on my own. I look up to God and say, "What am I supposed to do? Where do I get the money? I am doing the best that I can!" I feel a bit panicked.

The very same week as I am driving home from work, I get lightly tapped in the rear of my car. The damage is very minor but my car has a few scrapes. I am hit by a tow-truck, and the driver is nervous about the mishap. The driver doesn't want to go through insurance. He tells me to get an estimate and he'll pay me cash. He doesn't want his boss to know. His truck has no damage.

I get an estimate right away. Can you guess how much the estimate for the damage is? The damage total is $800.00. The cash is in my hand the day before I need to pay my car insurance. This accident I call a miracle. My car never gets repaired but I could care less. The car has close to 100,000 miles, and the damage is barely noticeable. This incident to me is a true Godsend. I don't worry about money again. Worry, you know, is a misuse of your imagination. Can you even imagine how grateful I am in this moment?

Very soon after the accident, my life really starts to take off. I know that as long as I do the best I can, I'll have what I need. When someone comes into the store with children that are the same age as my boys; without warning, the darkness just takes over me. But as long as I do all I can do, things just keep getting better. Some days the best I can do is to cry my eyes out. But each day gets a little better. I pray in gratitude every night that I made it through one more day, and continue to ask for guidance in making the choices that will take me in a positive direction. However, due to my past circumstances I still do not have confidence in myself to make good decisions.

After the car accident, with seeing how the money I need came to me, I do gain some confidence, and begin to believe I can make this new life work. I recognize God's help in all I do and can clearly see the advantage of the borrowed wings from above. My own strength is coming from within me somehow, because I know for sure my strength alone is not powerful enough to get me out of bed in the morning. My prayers are heard, and I witness their result every waking minute of my new life.

The year closes, and I barely make $17,000.00. With gratitude for all my blessings, I pray about my disappointment in finances, and let it go. The answer will come, and I believe I will have a better life soon.

The Hard Times

Living isn't so easy
When those that you hold dear
Move away, stay away
Year after year

Although my tears have faded
The emptiness is still a part
Of the lonely, longing feeling
That lives within my heart

Happiness comes from knowing
My loved ones are safe and warm
And the time we share together
Is spent in the most loving form

Memories of Happier Times 1975. left: Danny 1 year old, Jerome 2 1/2

It's difficult to turn the wheels of a parked car. But get it moving and you can guide it with just a touch. Whatever your dream, begin it. Boldness has genius, magic, and power steering in it.
Release your brakes!

- Edge Learning Institute

Chapter IV

Awakening To a New Dream

What about dreams when you sleep? Do you recall your dreams? Have you ever had the same dream repetitively? Do your dreams reveal any hidden meaning to you? My dreams have always provided me with plenty of insight. Since my early twenties with the help of several books, interpreting my dreams has proven to be quite helpful to me. Some dreams are just senseless mind-chatter, but others have given meaning and insight to my life.

One morning early in the second year of this new life, one of those insightful dreams comes to me. In this dream I am in a swimming pool by myself. The water is crystal clear. A bright sun is in the background with beautiful trees in full splendor all around. I feel glorious to be surrounded by such beauty. In the morning I tell my roommate about my dream and all the signs of success my dream reveals to me.

All three of the symbols, crystal clear water, sunshine, and trees full of healthy leaves, represent success and happiness, according to my dream books. Only one thing is wrong with this picture in my dream. In this dream I am fat. "What do you think it means?" I ask my roommate. We both look at each other and have a hearty laugh. Without any word exchange we move on with our day.

What comes next still baffles me. It's not at all what I expected. Smoking is a habit I'm not proud of but have no intention to quit at this point in my life. My first cigarette was at age thirteen. Managing to stop during pregnancies, it boggles my mind that I went right back to smoking afterwards. I know smoking is a bad habit, but it helps me through the day; at least that is what I tell myself. My roommate is also a smoker.

Not too long after the New Year begins, I receive one of those messages I refer to as a Godsend. While sitting, relaxing at home, lighting a cigarette, I take the first puff and notice a funny sensation in my body, accompanied by the thought to quit smoking. I say right out loud "You have got to be kidding!" But there is no response. No feeling, no thought, just silence. Knowing this message cannot be ignored, but not wanting to give up cigarettes, I just shake my head. No way! I feel a little angry, but know I have no choice but to surrender. I say out loud again, "Ok, but I need help with this one!" I am not happy about the new challenge given me.

To start, I cut back for a few weeks. Then I go cold turkey, with the understanding that not smoking will be a real blessing. In sales, smoking can be a real turn off when greeting a customer with smoky breath and reeking cloths, not to mention the health benefits gained. Now that I'm on a life path, to give up cigarettes is a better choice. However, I am still not happy about this task.

Eventually, I become grateful I heeded that message. On the other hand, I gain about fifteen pounds within the first three months. Can my dream of achieving success while being overweight, be coming true? I do not even have time to entertain that thought. The weight gain is the least of my concerns at the time.

I really do great in sales the first year. I earn the Sales Guild, which means I finish the year as one of the top 500 salespeople in the country with Volkswagen of America. Winners receive a weekend trip to a beautiful resort. It's been years since I've been away anywhere. I work with people that have been in sales for years and never achieved this level of success. I am so excited about this news, and I know I haven't accomplished this award on my own. I give thanks for all my blessings, especially these borrowed Wings that keep carrying me forward.

When the awards are announced, it becomes apparent that something isn't right with my paycheck. One pay period covers two weeks work, and during a two week period I sell and deliver ten cars. Ten cars is considered a great month at that time, let alone in two weeks. When my paycheck arrives, it is only $500.00, less taxes. This is low compensation even in 1988. To put ten cars on the road in that amount of time takes a lot of energy. Needless to say, I am very discouraged.

I begin contemplating leaving the business. I start to talk to some people. One person I know went to work at another dealership about fifteen miles away, and I call him to ask his opinion. He tells me I should at least try one more center before hanging up my hat. Pay plans are different, and he thinks I have the talent needed to succeed.

Before I even have the time to digest this information, I get a call from his boss. He invites me for an interview. I am hired on the spot. This center has the Volkswagen brand that I know already. The store appears to be a much more professional environment and also has a BMW franchise in the same building. My decision is quickly made to change locations.

When I give my notice to leave, both sales managers appear upset. A manager never wants to lose a good salesperson. These managers took the time to train me and did a great job. But as difficult as it is to leave, I make my decision. After my managers see I can't be swayed, they threaten me with "Once you leave, you cannot come back!" This creates deep emotions for me. I love working here. I have made many friends and the thought of leaving frightens me. Fear of the unknown.

On the other hand, the manager's resistance to my leaving really helps me to realize my value once again. Many salespeople have left there over the past sixteen months, and never did the managers fight to keep anyone else from walking out the door. I feel good about this fact, and I say my goodbyes. Off on a new adventure. This time I feel much better about a change because this change is my choice.

I need some new clothes. This new store demands an upscale look. I go shopping and apply for credit. I spend $700.00 and buy a few suits with all the trimmings. This is a big deal for me at the time and spending this amount of money makes me very nervous. The debt takes me years to pay off, but once I do, I never have credit card debt again.

The transition goes smoothly, and I get some more help from above. The very first week a young couple, Ted and Lisa Lips, come in. I had met them a few weeks earlier at my previous job. Ted and Lisa see me and laugh, "What are you doing here? We went back to see you, and you were not at the other store. We did not like the new salesperson so we decided to try this dealership." I explain I changed jobs and they reply, "It must be a sign we are meant to buy the car from you." I tell them I believe in signs. So, they sit down and buy a Volkswagen Jetta from me. Over the years, I sell them many, many cars. They also refer several of their friends to me. Ted eventually becomes my accountant.

I get off to a great start. My new job is very exciting and I start making more money immediately. At this point that's all I care about. I intend to get my own place to live for when my boys come to visit. That is all I live for, to spend time with them. This new job helps make my life a little easier by keeping my mind more occupied. This is a busier store with more floor traffic. Disciplining and training my mind helps me keep focus. This doesn't mean I don't cry myself to sleep many a night. Sometimes I just have to let the sadness out. But now I can repeat some of the games I used before to help me get through each day.

After a few weeks on the new job, I start getting phone calls from my previous manager. He tells me they changed the pay plan and he wants me back. He is adamant, calling me every day for weeks, then once a week for months. Once again I see my value, but I know I am in the right place.

Not long after I begin this new job, my children's father calls. He's remarried to a woman who has three children. He tells me if I want the boys in Catholic school, I need to pay half the tuition. So, I send him some money. The Catholic schools where he lives are the better choice. I am grateful for this new position that affords me the ability to help my children.

Also, my boy's father informs me of a grade school graduation party for my younger son Dan, and he invites me. This is the first time I meet his new family. The party creates a very uncomfortable and awkward situation for me. Tom introduces me to someone as his ex-wife. I pull him aside and quietly tell him, "Our marriage is annulled. I'm nothing to you anymore. I'm the mother of your children, so please introduce me that way."

At the party a friend of their family takes me under his wing. He makes me feel so comfortable. He says to me, "You know, it doesn't matter how much they do for those boys, (meaning Tom and new wife) the boys love for you shines right through. They light up every time your name is mentioned. Those boys love you so." "Thanks,

I appreciate your kindness" I reply. "We all shine when we are together. I live for our moments." He speaks the truth, and I know it. The joy shines through whenever we are together. This man helped me to see that I am not the only one who notices the love I share with my children. This party for Danny only cements in my mind the need to gain a better life to share with my boys.

With my new job, the goal of getting my own place takes no time at all. I move into a beautiful garden apartment that has a very nice pool and other amenities. This move gives me great comfort, to have a place I like, all my own. I am beginning to feel alive again. The circumstances of my life are still horrible to me, but at last I'm beginning to have a life I like and truly enjoy.

My older son, Jerome, joins the crew team at his high school and often rows about a half hour from where I live. I get to see him more often in the spring and summer months. Crew makes Sundays in the nice weather a real breather for all of us. We just hang out and enjoy a picnic lunch. Some days, this activity actually almost feels normal, just the three of us. Their father rarely comes. Of course I have to do all the driving back and forth, but I don't care one bit. The ride only gives me a few more hours with my sons.

Moving forward I embrace my job with enthusiasm. I choose happiness daily and find things to be grateful for every day. Gratitude is the key that keeps making things better in my life. Gratitude is the great multiplier. The more we are grateful, the more that comes our way. I am not aware of this fact at this point in my life. I only know that gratitude makes me feel better. In truth, I am genuinely grateful. I'm so much further ahead from where I began. My gratitude is real.

One memory I cherish happens one Friday night in spring. I am feeling very sad and down because it is Jerome's junior prom night. I feel I am missing something big in my sons' lives. My younger son

Danny is a freshman, and he has been invited by a girl he knows from the school play. My heart aches from not being there to share this moment with them. I make it home from work by 5:30 pm and give them a phone call. To my surprise, the phone call lasts until 7:00 pm. They pass the phone back and forth as they giggle and tease each other as young men do. I'm feeling their excitement as they put on tuxedos for the first time. Our conversation amazes me. I actually feel as if I am there with them. This act is a true gift from God, and my sons.

When we hang up the phone, I know they're going to walk down the stairs, take some pictures, and head out the door. I recognize this blessing immediately, and thank God. Never could I have imagined I would feel so good on this night. I feel so close to my sons. The memory of that night will warm my heart forever.

What comes next is something fantastic and totally unexpected. A few other salespeople and I are sent to a three-day seminar. I don't know what to expect. I'm thinking we will learn about cars and selling, but the seminar is totally different.

The Edge Learning Institute is behind the seminar which Volkswagen of America is sponsoring. The facilitator's name is Bob. He is like the energizer bunny. When he comes out, he just starts asking questions. Who here can ski? Some hands go up. Who here can build a bridge? Everyone just shrugs. He goes down a whole list of things. At the end he is screaming, wake up people! I did not ask if you HAVE done these things, I asked if you COULD!

YES! YOU CAN! You CAN do anything. ANYTHING! So, who can fly to the moon? Half the room puts up their hands, and he screams louder, WHO CAN FLY TO THE MOON? Waking up, the rest of the room raises their hands. By the end of the third day he throws a question like that out, and the whole room enthusiastically starts jumping up and down screaming, I CAN!!! I CAN!!!!

Bob plays the piano, tells us jokes and holds our interest all day long, while at the same time giving us very important information to think about. It's an experience I will not forget. It totally changes me. My experience lights pure passion in me. I have so much fun while at the same time soul searching. This seminar exhilarates me just thinking about it now. The workbook is alive with questions, and we have three full eight-hour days with time to explore our real desires.

A light switches on inside me, and I entertain the possibility of a new dream. Imagine that; A new dream. Just the thought of a new dream changes me instantly. Instead of just getting through the pain, making it through each day, I can actually aim for something. I never thought it possible for me to be excited about my life again. This awakening is a true miracle in my life, for sure.

Bob opens the door to new possibilities for the group. The whole room is buzzing with excitement. So what do I want? The only thing I had ever dreamt about since I was a child was being a mom and a homemaker. When the session ends, I am flooded with emotion. A new dream is a foreign idea to me. I listen to many people talk at dinner. The age group varies, and so do the goals each person discusses. All I can think is, "Can I really have another dream?" The possibility of a new dream is very strange to me, a new thought. I am uncertain about what I want.

After much thought and prayer I decide to set my sites on becoming a Sales Manager to gain a better lifestyle. I really enjoy sales and do quite well. I see the lifestyle my managers have. They support their families in a nice way. They get a demo among many other perks. Their duties are more diversified. They stay busier. In sales, there's a lot of down time, too much for me at this time in my life. Also, I wish to travel. The few places I've been with the Sales Guild opened my eyes to the fun of travel. So here is where my new dream begins to take shape. In this exact moment I begin to see a light at the end of the long, dark tunnel of sadness.

Next, we have to plan what the best course of action is to achieve our goals. I take it very seriously. I do the exercises in the workbook. The most important thing I learn during this seminar is that by the time I leave to go home, I ***believe.*** I **believe** I can have a new dream and achieve the goal. This is a very different feeling, very new for me indeed. This moment of ***belief*** is what really changes me on the inside. This possibility of a new dream is the first time since my earlier dreams were lost that I can even think about the possibility of a new dream. My brakes are now released.

Setting a goal for life is equal to setting a destination in the navigation system of a car. A destination must be plugged in before guidance can begin. Once a goal is set in life, or a destination in a car is set, all other elements must be in place. Engine on, fuel in the tank, eyes on the road, release the brakes, get moving, and of course follow the directions.

It's the same with us. We need to know what we want and where we wish to go; set a goal. We need to turn the engine on with intention, energize our actions with happiness, let go of all negatives which are the brakes, and follow the directions, and if we go off course or run into a detour, just get back on course as soon as possible.

So many people I see are just driving around with no destination in mind, just as I was, waiting for something to happen, just getting through the day. Don't wait. Whatever your dream, set the course. Begin now. You just might be amazed at how far you can go, and wherever you go, go happy. Happiness will get you to your destination faster.

At the seminar we receive a 5x7 card to take home with us that reads:

You rise or fall
Succeed or fail
By the image you hold
In your own mind

I place this right on the mirror of my dresser. I look at it every morning. Success is the image I hold in my mind. Yes, I can! Right in front of it, I place a much smaller card that was also given to us. It is a hidden picture of Jesus, one of those black ink prints. Some couldn't see the image. I saw it instantly. It is a reminder to me that Jesus is with me always, even if I don't see Him. So the image in my mind is success with Jesus in front. I am going to do all I can to be the best I can be. Now I am really enthused about my life.

I have a new game to play each morning. I see this card and imagine what I would do differently when I become a manager. I didn't think, 'IF' only 'WHEN.' How will I dress? What will I be thinking about when I am a manager? What kind of car will I be driving? These thoughts keep my mind busy in a fun way. The truth is I have no idea how to get into management, but the very thought of it helps keep me stay energized. This goal gives me a new focus. I believe this goal can be achieved even though I don't know how. Also, I imagine all the places I will travel with all the money I will make. Where will we go first? We, meaning my sons and I. Imagination can be a great tool when used the proper way. I imagined what a great life we would share.

At the seminar we also receive a small box of about thirty cards that have positive sayings and quotes on them, such as the one at the beginning of this chapter. I focus on one or two quotes a day, and for the first time in a long, long time, I become really excited about my life with all the possibilities. I start feeding myself positive thoughts daily.

In my down time, and there is plenty of down time on the sales floor, I sometimes sit and write affirmations. One day I must have written 'money just flows to me' about five hundred times. It was a very slow day! I usually write many different affirmations together, but for some reason this day I had a focus on money. When I go out to lunch on this particular day, I am driving on a four lane, major route in the left lane. All of a sudden I see money flying everywhere. I stop my car in the left lane. To my amazement there is no traffic around me. I get out of the car and start picking up as much money as I can grab as cash is flying about in the middle of the road. What a fun surprise.

After I collect the cash, I get back in my car and pull over to the shoulder. I look around to see if anyone is looking for the money. All of a sudden the traffic starts to flow again, as if magically timed for my safety. Not one person looks for the money. As I count the cash, I discover there is more than $100.00 that just flowed to me, and I recall my affirmations from earlier. Too bad I do not learn the lesson of how to rewrite my mental programming at this juncture of my life.

At this time there are only two salespeople on the BMW floor. I remember the advantage I had at my previous job working in both stores. I ask the sales manager, "If I learn the BMW product, can I take the overflow." He likes my ambition and says I can. There is not much overflow in this store, but every little bit helps.

I get out of my comfort zone once again. I feel alive. I have been dead inside for so many years that I am grateful to finally feel alive. Even though I am still somewhat detached inside, I now have hope for a new, happy life. My thoughts and beliefs are focused on success.

S *self-acceptance*
U *understanding*
C *caring*
C *concentration*
E *effort*
S *sharing*
S *staying power*

With this image in mind, and the belief that I can succeed, I do just that. In the year 1990, I not only make Sales Guild, I am now one of the Top 100 salespeople in the country for Volkswagen of America! This is a very big deal. With this honor comes an even longer trip to Las Vegas. I am so happy and excited. My success is hard for me to believe. In only four years I have gone from living on welfare to making $35,000.00. Plus, not only did I hit my target to travel, but I am now traveling for free. So, I experience the first win toward my new dream, and I feel great. My gratitude just keeps expanding because I know I did not achieve these things alone.

Not only do I go to Las Vegas, I also stay on an extra few days and go to the Grand Canyon. The trip is fabulous. I feel divinely guided and am so grateful for this new focus I have. My life still is not easy by any means, I work very hard and put in many long hours, but I feel that I achieved my first goal, and that feels good.

I still have the 'sadness' in me but I choose to look at what I have in the moment versus what is missing. I work hard at being positive. My focus is extremely difficult when building rapport with customers. People sometimes ask if I have any children. My situation is difficult for me to speak about. I become an expert at changing the subject. At this point I am still building the strength I need. I also still have a few people in my life to knock me down with constant challenges, but overall I am becoming stronger and more confident.

My life is improving slowly. This improvement is only because I choose to be happy and grateful every day. There's always something to be happy about if we look for it. To be grateful for breathing is a good place to start. *Happiness is not a destination; happiness is a means of transportation.* Someone said that to me early on in my sadness. 'Happiness is a means of transportation' took me years to fully understand, but once I grasped the meaning I put the concept to work in my life daily.

With this new goal in hand I begin to look for ways to get more information to bring my goal to me. I ask my boss questions about what he is doing and why. I become curious about procedures I'd never thought of before. I ask myself questions about how I might handle a situation. Or how could I make a process better? I begin to look at things differently. I wonder what questions I should be asking of myself. How far can I go? What more should I be doing? How can I do better? What do I need to learn?

I understand that all of us are a work in progress. I am determined to be the best I can be. So, I pray for awareness of what I need to know. What are the questions I need to ask? The answers really do come if you ask the questions. *Ask and you shall receive.*

If you aren't that in tune with yourself to get the needed answers, ask someone close to you. Ask them what they think you need to do to get to a goal, or to be a better person. Ask your husband or wife if you are living up to your potential. You need to be open to the truth. You cannot get better at something if you aren't aware what you lack.

Also, in sales it's always good to know your intention before you make a call or speak with a customer. What is the goal or intention for the phone call or customer visit? Am I going for an appointment? Providing information? Building rapport? Following up? Being aware of the intention gives focus and direction. In life, an intention works the same way. Once a goal is set, an intention placed before any action will bring focus and intensify the action.

My daily intention is to do the very best I can and make the best choices possible. This prayer becomes a constant in my life, "Thank You for helping me make the choices that will bring me closer to You." This is my daily mantra. I know life is all about choices. I intend to make the best choices for the best life I can possibly have in the future. And guess what? I believe I do just that.

I give the best I can wherever I am in the moment. I keep my goal in my mind. To become a manager, I clearly need to learn more and gain more experience, but am not sure where to get the information I need. The fact is there is so much information out there. If you don't know what you need, want, or what is holding you back, you will never get anywhere. I know the experience will come if I remain curious about the details at work, and stay focused on the job at hand. There are so many books to read on management, I am stifled. What is the best information for me? So, I pray for guidance.

Many people at the same seminar with me were very excited when we left, but after a few days I saw them go right back into their comfort zones. Nothing changed for them. This I didn't understand. The way I see things, life begins when you exit your comfort zone. That has been my experience in life. My old boss used to joke that some people come to work and say, 'I hope and pray I sell a car today.' Then they sit and wait. It takes more than prayer. Prayer is a great place to start, but reaching goals also requires intelligent, intended actions.

What is holding you back? Ask the question of yourself. You will get an answer if you are willing to receive it. I believe many people fear change. Many are stuck in a rut just waiting for someone or something to come along and make them happy. This is it folks. What are you waiting for? Happiness is your choice.

This is it!
Get excited!
This is your life
Don't wait to be invited!

If ever I feel stuck, I ask the question. "What do I need to do? What am I not seeing?" It's the questions we ask ourselves that drive our lives and the results we get. Life is what we make it. Sometimes if I am really down or stuck, and believe me I have my days, I just say, "I need a leg up out of this mess, please!" Asking for help usually gets the job done. But awareness is the key. We need to know where we are in the present moment to get the help we need.

Many days I just don't feel like doing the work I need to do. Some days I just want to give in and let the sadness have me. The sinking feeling of giving up comes over me. These are the days I just go through the motions. Usually, once I start my day, my spirit takes over and my focus changes. To get into motion is the key. Just get a move on. The power steering in a car does not kick in until the engine is on and the motion begins.

When I look back to this time, I realize that once I set a direction and held the **belief** I could do it, life just kept directing me to what I needed to do. I did follow the directions and did all I could. I didn't need to know how my future goal would arrive, I only needed to ***believe and act accordingly.***

The answer to my prayer for more knowledge comes almost immediately. Tony Robbins visits the area for a two day seminar, and the dealership sends me to see him. Tony Robbins is a big name in the motivation world, and author of many books. He is an awesome presence on stage. His energy just radiates to the audience.

These educational events are such a great gift to me. I love this information. Tony inspires me in many ways. The information he shares sheds light on more areas I need to work on, which is exactly what I asked for in my prayer. The group receives workbooks and I get right down to business. Tony Robbins gives us some great information.

I learn more about the psychology behind the art of persuasion, and receive some really great tips that help me communicate in a more effective way. He speaks about the Power within us and techniques on how to harness this Power. He teaches us how to study ourselves to learn how to turn ourselves on instantly when needed. Much like an athlete does before a game. Just this one tip helps me make more sales immediately.

Some days at work when I'm sitting for hours before a customer walks in, I find difficulty being motivated and enthused. Not now. I study my behavior when in an excited state, and now can go right into that body position, do the same gestures and BAM! I am in a motivated state. This knowledge makes a huge difference in my sales.

Once again, I feel charged. I put some of the things I learn right to work. I can measure my progress immediately. My communication skills become fine-tuned. I instantly am able to read people better and pick up the body signs they are sending my way. I also become aware of my own signals and body language. This information puts more steam in my engine to get to my goal faster, and I am excited.

Many people seem disinterested at the seminar and complain that they are missing a day on the sales floor. I am in disbelief. This information isn't just for sales. This information can be used in daily life. Who doesn't want to improve? The ideas Tony speaks about require getting out of your 'comfort zone,' and too many people are just satisfied to stay in their rut, even when they aren't happy. I just wanted to shout at some people and say, "WAKE UP!"

Are you in a rut? Do you understand what your beliefs are? Do you ask yourself any questions? This is your life and only you have control over what you think and feel. You can have life your way. A goal is needed to get directions. Do you have a goal set? Are you clear about what you desire? You can have whatever you desire.

As the year moves on for me, I am working many hours. The days are mostly nine to nine with a night off if I am lucky. Saturday is eight-thirty to six. Never are there two days off in a row. I have one day off during the week and Sunday. Selling cars definitely is hard work. The job keeps me busy and focused, and for this I am grateful. I become so inspired by my new goal I don't care what it takes from me, I will succeed.

By now Jerome is heading off to college. I am so grateful that I am in a position to pay half his tuition. I take him on a shopping spree for some new clothes. He is boarding at school only about two hours away. Danny and I get to visit often.

By the end of 1991 I make the TOP 100 salespeople list again with Volkswagen, an incredible achievement. There is also a program in place where I have about $20,000.00 earned from the manufacturer in an account that will be paid quarterly over the next three years. This program is designed to keep sales people with the brand. I am able to start collecting the first quarter of 1992. This will be paid on top my commissions which amounted to over $35,000.00 this past year. I now feel like I am on top of the world. I really feel good about my life, and wonder "Can my life get any better?" My imagination is working overtime, how much better can my life get? What will the New Year bring? Little do I know that God has more changes for me ahead, so please come along and see how these changes affect me.

Now

The time has come, the time is now
No time to sit and wonder how
Just do or die, bare face, don't lie
Make up your mind, and don't ask why

There's nothing to it but to do it
Sometimes though we look right through it
If nothing ventured is nothing gained
Nothing gained is a loss sustained

No one can do it for you
Take the time to look inside you
Then get up off your behind
Get the light inside you to shine

Are we having fun yet?
Everyone has a sure bet!
There's nothing to it but to do it
Like Nike says; "Just do it!"

You gotta do what you gotta do
No apologies, no excuses
You gotta do what you gotta do
Only you control your mind's uses

Prom Night left: Danny right: Jerome

The energy derived from setting goals comes in large part from the focus it brings to our lives. It's like igniting a fire by channeling the gentle rays of the sun to a single spot through a magnifying glass.

- Edge Learning Institute

Chapter V

A Change of View

As the New Year starts, to my surprise the owner adds another franchise. He opens a Dodge dealership. When the Dodge store opens in the beginning of 1992, a new management team comes on board also. This three-man team changes the existing selling system. I go through the training with an open mind, although I don't like how it sounds. The selling system this team brings is totally different in every way from how the current sales team handles a sale. To me this new system appears to talk down to the customer.

When put into action this new system is just horrible. Basically, I must ask each customer upon entering the store if he is here for the BIG SALE when in reality there is no BIG SALE. Then, I proceed to show him the car but do not negotiate price. The manager comes out to handle all negotiations.

The new process appears easy enough until the manager comes out and speaks to the potential buyer as if the buyer is stupid. My first potential customer doesn't even respond to him. He looks me in the eyes and says, "Thanks Terri, you were very nice, but I refuse to talk to this idiot!" and he walks out. "Oh, no! This can't be good," I think to myself. What now? This three-man team is not polished enough for this neighborhood or for the import buyer. Dodge customers are very different, and this management team came from another Dodge dealership in Pittsburgh. This is a very affluent, well-educated customer base on the Mainline of Philadelphia. These customers are not going to be lead blindly into a sale, and this is what this selling system is set up to do. I am at a loss and am not sure what I can do.

In the meantime, a new Cadillac store in town has been calling me and offering me a job. I go to speak to them about the position. The facts are unclear about how much money I can make because this is a new store, and there is no telling how many cars this point will produce or what the average profit range will be to base an estimated commission. This job is very risky. I would have to walk away from all I have worked so hard for. I will lose the $20,000.00 I already earned to be paid over the next three years, and the trip I just earned. I have to make a tough decision and one I don't care to make.

I don't want this change. I was thrilled with the way things were two weeks ago. At the same time I feel sick inside to be forced to say the things this new management team wants me to say. My emotions are going crazy. I know I have to calm down to get clear direction. I know that a cool, calm center is needed for clear direction from my Divine navigation system. In this moment, I am too emotional.

You need to be open and clear to receive direction. If you are jammed up inside holding onto anger or any of the other negative feelings, you cannot receive a clear signal. It's like having static on a radio. You must find a way to get back to your calm. For certain I am jammed up. My emotions are on a roller coaster ride. I feel angry that things have to change right when I am doing so well. I decide to take a few days off so I can get clear. I find the situation I am in hard to believe. How is this happening right when everything was going great? I speak to some friends, but know ultimately this decision is mine. Of course, I pray for direction.

While I am off from work the Cadillac store ups their ante by offering me a guarantee of at least $30,000.00 for the first year. Being a new store the owner doesn't know what the year will produce. The guarantee gives me a good feeling. To know I am valued by the owner gives me such assurance. This guarantee is less than I made last year but is good enough to live a decent life. Any guarantee is rare in the car business, especially for sales people. This offer is something I need to consider.

I had worked with the manager at the Cadillac store previously, so he knows my strengths. I am at a loss for what to do. I must think and pray on it. I only wish things could go back to the way they were. But this is not how life works, and I must decide. Don't fight the tide. I have confidence the way will be shown to me.

When I go back to work I become aware that a few more negative episodes had occurred in my absence. One of my customers came in to buy a car and did not like the way the manager spoke to him. I lost another sale. I spoke to the gentleman on the phone, and he apologized to me because he knows I spent time with him. He bought the same car from another dealer due to the fact he will not do business with my manager. This is someone I have worked with for weeks to find the right car. I see the light and have my answer. I give my notice and pack up my desk.

To leave this job is much more difficult because I have put so much energy into the last four years. Walking away hurts. The owner appears to be as upset as I am. He doesn't want me to go. I explain my reason but he feels I should give it more time. He believes this management team he hired will prove true in the long run. I do not share his same vision.

The Volkswagen factory rep is in shock when he hears the news that I quit. He doesn't believe I am leaving because I have the largest amount of money in my account for the next three years than anyone in his territory. The whole purpose of the program is to keep people like me. I tell him this hurts me more than it hurts him. I explain that I will not put myself into a situation where I feel I am compromising who I am. This new system does not feel right to me, and to say and do the things this new team requires of me, is not for me. I don't want to go. I've asked the new manager if I can please just stay and sell cars the way I have done in the past, and he refuses. So, out the door I go.

To have so many people upset over my leaving does make me feel good. I have seen so many people come and go in this business. No one ever bats an eye. Once again, my value is illuminated. However, at this moment, the sadness of leaving the job I love overrides all the good feelings of seeing my own value.

The Cadillac store is just opening, and there are very few customers walking through the door. I experience more down time than ever before. The days seem longer, even though we close an hour earlier. The people who work here are great. We have a lot of fun playing pranks on each other and playing stupid games. Even the owner gets involved in our childish play. Our playful delights help keep spirits high during the down time.

The one game we play is so funny that I still laugh when I think of it. Someone bought a small "Mr. Bill" doll, about five inches tall. Every day someone in our group kidnaps the doll and hides it somewhere. Pictures taken with a Polaroid camera along with a ransom note cut out from magazines will show up during the day to give clues as to who has the doll and what danger "Mr. Bill" is facing. This game goes on for months if not the entire year, and some of the photos and notes are just hysterical and very time consuming to make, but the game keeps us all laughing when we have no work to do.

The challenge of this job is not enough for me, but I never look back. I know the direction came from my Divine navigation system. I am on the right path. I do all I can to look at the bright side. I make the most of the situation at hand.

My son Jerome is in need of a car and I am able to buy him an old Volkswagen Rabbit that still has lots of life. I buy the car through a wholesaler that buys old cars from the Cadillac store. The car needs a bit of clean up, and I pay our detailer to work on it after hours. The Rabbit shines up beautifully and creates a happy moment for me and my son. I am able to give my son some independence. That little VW lasted Jerome many years.

With my management goal in mind, I ask my boss to show me some of what he does, such as ordering cars, appraisals, advertising, and anything else he can think of to teach me. He enjoys negotiating and he bargains with me. He'll show me some of what he does if I take all his product tests for him. I am the product specialist! I know everything inside and out. This is an easy task for me, plus this task helps me fill in some of the long, down time hours.

My boss shows me the computer system where he orders the cars, very antiquated from today's standards. I also see the tools he uses for appraising trade-ins. This man has a true talent in the way he speaks to customers. He's able to sit down and converse with anyone in a relaxing manner. I learn a lot from him in this area of the job.

One funny experience I have at the Cadillac store, actually kind of sad when I reflect, is with an older gentleman who comes in to buy a car. It's my turn to greet the customer and I welcome him in my usual manner. He seems to be a bit defensive so I lighten my approach with him. This tactic doesn't help. Every time I take a step closer to him, he steps away. Like two magnets repelling each other. The scene becomes almost comical. Finally, after about five minutes, he runs over to a salesman sitting at his desk and announces, "I don't want to talk to no broad." The other salesman takes over. The man proceeds to buy a car on the spot. The easiest sale in history! This kills me because I can use the commission, but I just have to laugh. It takes all kinds.

As the year closes, I finish the year with Sales Guild. Earning Sales Guild elates me because I did not think I had a chance this year. It has only been eleven months since I began with Cadillac, and to reach Guild level is no easy task. Winning Sales Guild earns me a trip to Las Vegas! This in my mind makes up for the trip to Las Vegas I gave up when I left my last job. The guarantee proves to be a real blessing also. I did not come close to earning $30,000.00 with my commissions alone. I'm very grateful for the way the year turns out, even though this is still a step back financially.

Another God sent blessing is that Cadillac pays many rewards with all kinds of points. Points equal cash on catalog purchases. I am able to get many household items. The best is a Tunturi treadmill that I still have today. Also, I manage to get a set of luggage for all the traveling I'm set on doing, a TV, pots and pans, canisters, an expensive handbag, and lots of gift cards to restaurants and other franchise stores. Overall, it is a very good year. With my guarantee and all the perks, I do just fine. 1992 ends on a grand note.

In 1993 everything gets better in my personal life. My son Dan calls me and says, "My bags are packed, come and get me!" He graduated from high school and decides to go to college in my area, mainly so we can live together. I am in heaven. He hates being apart as much as I do.

I made it through the sadness! I am clear. The clouds are passed, and I can see the sunshine. I'm so very pleased with the effort I put into the past several years. Now I have a real life to share with my son. I see the benefit of my actions. I thank God every day for carrying me through the pain. I'm so elated in the moment my feet are not even touching the ground. Off I go to get my son. What a glorious day it is.

I am feeling great. Finally! So proud of the choice I made to be happy no matter what, keeping myself clear enough to receive direction. Accepting what is, instead of fighting it. I can see how by doing that I am in this great situation today. I am so grateful at this point for all the help from above. The borrowed wings got me through. Thank You, Lord!

In August of 1993 my family had to say good-bye to my dear mother. To lose her at this time makes me sad because she never really got to witness me live my joy and I know that is all she ever wished for me. I am so grateful for all she taught me and for her unconditional love. In writing this book I discovered just how brilliant a mother she was and how her influence has shaped my life. God bless you, mom.

One day I go home and find several messages on the answering machine for Dan. He is making friends fast and I am so happy to see him adjust so easily. When he gets home, I give him the messages and ask him who his best friend is. He looks at me with a strange look and says, "You, mom. You're my best friend." He just melts my heart. I am his mother, but the truth is over the years of separation we did become great friends, and for this I am very grateful.

The adjustment we make to living together is easy and unforced. He works part-time while he attends college which is only about twenty minutes from where we live. I am able to buy him a used car through a wholesaler, also, and he too has the freedom he needs. I have not felt this happy in years. I wake up in the morning, and I feel so free. The weight of the sadness is gone. Everyone I know notices the difference in me. I am not just happy, I am living in joy.

My financial year is about the same as the year before. I make maybe a few thousand more and of course the Sales Guild along with another trip to Las Vegas. When I return home from the Vegas trip in mid-May, I receive a phone call from my previous manager. He asks if I would like to be the Volkswagen Sales Manager at my previous location. What? Are you kidding me? I don't even have to think about this one. The job's potential is double the money I earn now, plus a demo to drive, and 100% car and health insurance coverage. Out of the clear blue! I go and speak with the owner to firm up the details. The owner is as delighted as I am. He's very excited to get me back on his team. Imagine that. I have arrived at my destination.

I am in awe of the situation. I have attained my goal without even knowing how to get there. All my hard work now pays off. The way management came to me just blows me away. All I can do is say thank you, Lord! Had I not made the move to Cadillac, this promotion would not be happening. It's rare for good salespeople to be promoted and taken off the sales floor. They are too hard to replace.

When I give my notice at the Cadillac store, both my manager and the owner are very upset to say the least. They both try at length to change my mind, but nothing they say can change my decision. This is my dream! When I tell my manager the pay plan I will be working under, he almost chokes. That's about the same as I make! "They really do want you back to offer that pay without any experience," he says.

My Management position begins in June of 1994. Yes, I can! Yes, I did. I am so very grateful for this opportunity and happy I took the risk to leave. To arrive at this goal is definitely by Divine Guidance. I had no clue this is where I was heading. Not in my wildest dreams. I just did the best I could with the job in front of me and kept the vision of my goal in mind. I chose to be happy right where I was in the moment.

I see the results of my prayer and know the reason I pray. My life is always guided this way, and even when I cannot see where I am going, BAM! I arrive at a goal. Woowhooo!!! Trust in God has led me here. The Universal vision can see so much more than we can; the all-seeing eye. You need to set a goal in order to receive directions.

My dreams and goals become reality. I did it! I am so happy with my life now, especially that Danny is home with me. Nothing can top this feeling I have. It is well beyond the best result that I could ever hope for. I have made my way through the sadness. I wake up every morning now with true joy in my heart. I am alive and discover the most wonderful time in my life. I appreciate the life I have every second of every day.

What happened in my life that allowed this miracle to happen? I have to ask this question so I can understand and learn. I realize that nothing changed in my life until I ***accepted*** the fact that my past dream was gone. I had to let go of my lost dream and ***accept*** the fact I needed to walk through the pain. Even during my sadness and pain I found many things to be happy and grateful for in my life. I am also grateful for the strength I received from above. I recognize this blessing and know I did not get through the sadness and pain alone. I could not have made this journey on my own power. This I know for sure.

For as long as I can remember I've kept a journal. However, not until I started keeping a ***gratitude*** journal did things really begin to improve. Focusing on the positive helped me put one foot in front of the other and do all I can with what is in front of me. Most of all though, I ***believe***. I believe in myself, keep myself positive, and trust God to guide me. I have to say thank you to the "Oprah Show," where I learned about the positive effect of keeping a gratitude journal. Prior, my journals logged much of the sadness I felt. To log the gratitude daily really helped me *focus on the positive,* and make a difference in my life. Thanks, Oprah.

What I can see clearly now is that while living in the 'sadness,' I was unable to move forward until I ***accepted*** that my dream was gone.

As much as I hurt, as much as I hated it, I was just dying inside. I had to let go of the anger. I had to let go of my past dream, the pain of losing that dream, and the pain of missing my children. I had to ***accept*** my life as it was in order to move on.

Because I took way too long to let go, I'm sharing my story with you. The sooner you can ***accept*** whatever is holding you back, the sooner you can start to get better. Do you even know what is holding you back? If you are holding on to past pain, anger, forgiveness issues, guilt, hate, or fear, let go and move into the positive. Please do not allow your past to ruin your present moment.

I feel as if I have lived "Murphy's Law." Everything that could have gone wrong for me did, and at the worst possible time. But what I do discover in my life is that once I get through all the negatives, it's ***positive*** all the way. I have to really dig deep to discover my truth. Make yourself aware of just what you are holding on to inside.

At this point in my life I still have something big holding me back. I don't yet know it's a limiting belief. I think this belief is a fact of life, a truth I will reveal to you later in my journey. In the meantime, here are some more thoughts that carry me through.

Dreams

Dreams are made for living
Dream on and continue giving
Reality is a dream come true
So when you dream, leave room for you

Dreams are positive all the way
Keep that in mind then be on your way
Believe in yourself, be happy for today
Dream your dream, and energize your day

Every day is a new start. Start out fresh. In my neighborhood the trash gets picked up twice a week. How about where you live? Have you ever missed a day? It is amazing how fast trash can pile up. The trash I am speaking of here, however, is your own personal trash. I see so many people holding onto events that are long gone. The personal garbage needs to be taken out on a regular basis. Don't allow yesterday's trash to take up space inside of you. Garbage does you no good and only stinks up your life, literally.

Personal trash can pile up fast if we don't pay attention, guilt for something we did or didn't do, anger over what someone did to us, worry about finances or our job, any and all of those negatives that weigh us down. Learning to take out the trash by letting go of any negative experiences at the end of the day enhances your life immensely. Examine the negative feeling, analyze the feeling if you must, and then put it in the trash. Next, contemplate something positive that happened that day; there is always something positive if you look for it. Feeling positive also enhances sleep.

It takes practice to achieve 'trash free' living, but the reward of doing so is well worth the effort. To start out fresh each day ***feels so good.*** When all the negative feelings are gone, there is so much more room for the good feelings, and when you feel good…good things happen.

Many health problems and diseases are now being connected to negative feelings such as anger, resentment, and the largest contributor, stress. So learning to let go of all these negatives the best we can will help us all live happier, healthier lives. Every feeling we have generates a frequency, and that is why those negative feelings are not good for us. Holding onto resentments, or not forgiving someone creates a negative frequency inside of us and, therefore, only hurts us.

I can see clearly how my life really took off with the birth of a new dream. All things are now possible. You need to be happy now to start the process where you are. Don't wait for some event or some person to be happy. Begin your dream now. Be happy right where you are today. Talk about things you love and wish to do. Talk about the life you desire to have. But be happy right where you stand now. Choose to be happy in the moment, no matter what, and your life will improve. Your smile awakens and releases the joy inside you, so don't hold back. Share a smile and feel good.

There is a song I love from "South Pacific" called "Happy Talk."

Some of the lyrics are as follows:

Happy, happy, happy, happy talk
Talk about things you like to do
If you don't have a dream
Then how you gonna have a dream come true?

So please come along and see just how my dream of being a Sales Manager develops. There are still many surprises ahead.

Be Happy

Be happy, no matter what
Or you put yourself in a rut
Your life will never offer you less
When you plant a seed of happiness

Be grateful for what you have today
How much or how little varies each day
But all equals nothing when it's taken away
Aim high, reach far; be happy where you are today

Happiness can only come from within
We seldom are happy about every little thing
But there's always something to find and begin
Just be happy for today, and you are sure to win

Put happiness in your life today
Put all resentments out of the way
Make it a habit to dump them each day
Then start fresh with each and every new day

Cousin David's Wedding 1996 left: Jerome, Terri, Dan

You live longer once you realize that any time spent being unhappy is wasted

- Ruth E. Renski

Chapter VI
Glory Days

Do you have a goal? Do you have a dream? My dream life is now beginning and I am not even sure how I arrived. I did have a goal in mind but had no clue how to get there. I pray every day and watch for signs and/or direction. I do the best I can, and before I know it, my dream life arrives. Many people I know are just drifting either because they do not know what they want, or because they feel their goal is out of their reach. Let me tell you a secret: nothing is out of God's reach. All you have to do is allow God to give you directions, and there is no end to the possibilities.

The date now is June, 1994. I am so happy and excited. Is this really my life? Here is my dream delivered. Now, what do I do? I receive no training or instruction, not one person to tell me what to do. Whatever I lack in know-how, I certainly make up with enthusiasm. My feet hardly touch the ground my spirits are so elevated.

The sales team is already in place. No one is left in sales that I know from prior years. This sales team has no idea who I am and live in fear of the unknown. I have the ability to make their lives miserable. In sales, the two scariest changes are a change in pay plan or a change in management. I have a real challenge before me. I pray for guidance.

My home life is fantastic. Danny is in college and just to see him every day is such a treat, a feeling beyond compare. We get together with Jerome as often as we can. The biggest difference to me now is that I wake up every day excited to be alive. My eyes open and look with glee to the day ahead. There is no more challenge to keep my mind busy. I am totally happy and grateful. There is no fight to be happy anymore. What a wonderful life I have. I always knew the sadness would end one day but never imagined my life to be so happy.

My job now is to motivate and manage others, and of course to sell cars, a job I can do easily with the way my happiness overflows. Happiness is contagious, and my life is living proof. Once the sales team sees that I am for real and really care, they begin to pay attention. When they discover I am willing to do anything to help them, they come alive and begin to trust me. There have been many 'big shot' managers working at this dealership, managers that just sat back and gave orders. The sales team can see I'm all about getting involved. They respond to me in a positive way. We start cooking with sales right away. My enthusiasm and happiness are over the top and infiltrates the entire atmosphere.

My first month in management is one of the most exciting months of my whole career. We shatter the store's record. We deliver fifty cars when the month's goal was set at only thirty. I make sure we celebrate each sale, and the excitement becomes electric. With all the excitement we become a solid team. To have gained the trust of this sales team really makes me feel great. I came into this job knowing the owner trusted me, but now I have all the confidence I need.

For months I am elated. I love every minute of the long, long days. Most days last from nine in the morning to nine at night, and many nights even later. Hours total between sixty to seventy hours a week, depending if I work on my day off and how many nights I stay after closing. The hours make for a long week, but my excitement and enthusiasm carry me through.

There are three managers, one for each franchise: VW, BMW, and Dodge. The BMW manager also handles the used cars, and he is the person who put my name in the hat when the store needed a new manager. He is my previous manager, before the three-man team came on-board, and a good friend. The three of us cover each other for our days off, which are rare. We all put as much effort as we can into our own departments to get the profits up. Dodge has been a real challenge since the doors opened in 1992 and has drained the resources.

Nothing can get me down at this point in my life, not even the long hours. I'm sure many people tire of my positive anecdotes, but I cannot help myself, I see the positive in everything. The enjoyment I experience in my life now is incredible. Gratitude fills my being from the moment I wake up until the end of the day. My energy seems endless. To see my son in the morning is a miracle to me. From sadness, I now live in joy. No more trying to find something to be happy about. I am happy about everything, all the time. My energy soars in leaps and bounds. My happiness radiates. My mind and spirit are free from the chains the sadness placed on me for so many years.

I learn very quickly all the aspects of this new role as manager. I enjoy the entire process. I love the meetings I attend where the management staff plans ahead. We set strategies for a business plan, discuss profits and ways to improve, plan sale dates, review employees, discuss customer issues and plan advertising, all topics new and very exciting to me.

Many meetings held are with the service and parts departments, and I learn how the back-end of the business runs. This is all new to me. I've always been aware of the basics in regard to that end of the business, but in these meetings I get to learn many more aspects, especially how my sales and projected sales affect the rest of the store. Sales projections are new to me, and now that I understand how my projections affect the service and parts departments, I become a bit nervous. My monthly projections let the service department know how many hours of labor time they need to hold aside for new car preps. The parts department bases its stock dollars based on my projections. If I am wrong, my projection has the potential to cost the dealership a lot of money.

To project a clear and true sales target is no easy task for me. Having plowed past the stores record my first month, all the averages go right out the window. I approach the owner for some insight when my first sales projection is due, and all he can do is laugh and say, "That's why I hired you. You are the manager now, so give it your best shot. If I knew the answer, I would not need you!" He laughs for days about my question.

As time goes on, I learn how to make the best projection I can. This task never gets easier for me, but I gain the confidence I need, and I give it my best shot every month. With increasing sales no one really gets hurt if I am off a little. I learn that with increasing sales any and all mistakes are mostly overlooked, but with decreasing sales the mistakes are magnified, if not imagined. An increase in sales overrides most negatives.

My Volkswagen representative is the same man that was so upset when I left the sales team to go to Cadillac. He is also a good friend of mine and gives me more advice during my learning experience as a manager than anyone in the dealership. From his budget he runs several contests a year for managers, and the manufacturer also offers a few trips as rewards for successful managers. These awards always offer great vacation packages, mostly long weekends to some fabulous resort in the United States. These trip incentives help build excitement, as if I needed help in that department.

The award trips are offered as extra vacation time from the dealership, which is a big deal to me because of all the hours I work. The long hours had served my life well during the sad years, but now that I am in a happy place, I'd love to have more time off. I never enjoyed the long, tedious hours of the car business but realize the blessing they were in past days. But now, besides gaining a free trip, the extra time off gives me an added drive to win.

At the launch of one of these award trip contests, the manufacturer sends out a brochure with the destination intended for the winners, and this package includes the activities offered on the trip. I take the brochure and draw myself in the picture somewhere, either lying on the beach, or hanging out a window of the hotel designated in the brochure. I make just a stick drawing of myself, but I put the words "Here I am" coming out of my mouth. I put the brochure on the bulletin board in my office. I see the brochure every day for three months and I say, "Yes!" every time it catches my attention. So guess what? I win almost every trip. Now, I not only attain my goal of travel, but I am traveling for free. My life is just over the top with splendor, not to mention all the extra days off during the year.

Even with all of the management's efforts, profits are not as good as we expected. The building is old and is in need of many upgrades. Right now BMW and VW share a showroom, a very large showroom with a divider in the center, but not good enough to meet our manufacturer's standards. The manufacturers are putting pressure on owners for stand-alone facilities. There is a point where our BMW center is almost sold, but luckily it does not come to that point.

In 1995 a business partner comes on board. He seems friendly, and evidently has the money to put in the necessary upgrades. Money has been a real struggle for the current owner over the past few years. The Dodge franchise is not doing well and actually hurts our customer base with BMW, not to mention the hardship this brand placed on the dealer's relationship with BMW. The Dodge brand did more damage to this store than any profit it brought. Not so much due to the brand itself, but more because of timing, the management team in place, and location for the brand. This is not the proper neighborhood for the demographics of the Dodge brand. The damage caused to the relationship with BMW takes years for the owner to recover.

With this new partnership, the current Dodge manager sees the writing on the wall and the direction the Dodge franchise is going, and he quits for a better opportunity. The owner has so much confidence in me he decides to give me the Dodge store to handle on top of my current Volkswagen management job. This may sound like a promotion but is not the best choice in my opinion. The brands are very different, and so are the customers. But to save money, and the cost of another manager, the Dodge and Volkswagen showrooms are combined, and I inherit another team to oversee along with another brand to manage. The change creates more work for me, but I am still so far above the ground, I handle the situation as best I can.

To combine the showrooms is much easier than combining the two sales forces. Each team is trained in its own product and many are not open to learning the other brand (that comfort zone I mentioned earlier). This creates confusion on the floor because all customers enter by the same door. Eventually, I demand the salespeople gain the knowledge they need to sell both products. Only one problem remains. Many of the sales team that originated with the Volkswagen brand, threaten me by saying, "If I have to speak to one more Dodge customer, I will quit!" I cannot tell you how many times I hear this mainly because the demographic is so different and the American brands have many more upgrade 'packages' that takes more time to explain properly. From a selling perspective, Volkswagen is much easier to explain.

During these several years in management I learn many new skills. With a new partner on board, the store needs to get the message out so the neighborhood will come back to shop. We look for an advertising agency to represent us, and this brings along some fun. Three different advertising firms are called to give us proposals. I enjoy being a part of this process. Creative people are such fun to work with. Each company has different approaches, but the creative teams all work in a similar fashion. Each team comes in separately and asks me many different questions. Then they go to work to create a campaign on the info they gathered. I really enjoy seeing my ideas incorporated into an ad campaign. All of the proposals are very good.

We vote and discuss the pros and cons of each proposal, and then choose the one we like the best. Out into the world our ideas go. I now have to come up with ads every week and measure the results to see what works best. Not all results are easy to measure, and once again I learn a great deal. At this time the newspaper is a major player in advertising, very different from today's world and the internet frenzy.

Other major, personal experiences happen during this period. My dad gets very sick this year. I get to visit as often as I can but am working so many hours it makes it difficult to get to see him as often as I would like. Towards the end of his life, my sister Eileen calls to say dad does not have much time left. In the middle of a busy day I tell my boss I am taking an extra-long lunch to sneak a quick visit with dad. He is about a forty minute drive each way if the traffic is not congested. When I arrive to visit, all my sisters just happen to be there also. This is not planned but appears to be. My dad looks up, sees us all and says, "It's not going to be today," as if we are all standing there waiting for him to die. That is my dad, always a sense of humor.

In September, 1995, dad joins my mom in heaven. Again, I count the blessings this man gave me, and the unconditional love. I am forever grateful for the love we shared, and that he did get to witness me live in joy before he passed. I owe the strong roots of faith, family, and love to my parents. God bless them both.

Back on the job front, it's business as usual. A salesman comes into my office one day to check-out before his customer leaves, which is the normal protocol. He reports his customer is going to buy a car when she finds a job. She is relocating to the area, and is looking for work. I ask, "What kind of work is she looking for?" The salesman is not sure. Interesting, I think. I go and speak with her and I discover she is a lovely person. We speak about the possibility of her selling cars. The thought intrigues her although she is very reluctant at first. After a few meetings, she takes the job and learns fast. She also buys a Volkswagen Jetta just as she promised.

Once trained, she turns into an excellent salesperson, and eventually becomes a friend. At this juncture, my earlier dream of being successful and overweight is now true. My clothes are two sizes larger than ever before. This new sales woman keeps showing me pictures of the 'before' and 'after' photos of people in magazines that have lost weight. A light goes on once again in my mind; I need to lose weight. The saleswoman does not recall this gesture today, and may not have shown me the articles with intention, but somehow I received the message I was meant to see in those magazines. That is how God speaks to me.

I set a new goal to lose twenty-five pounds. I start to pack my lunch and dinner instead of eating take out. I start an exercise regimen. Up to this point, fast food was the norm for lunch and most times dinner. My focus has been on the job for so long. I need a better life plan. Now is the time to make a change.

I stop drinking soda, begin to plan meals ahead, and use portion control. Before long I am down about fifteen pounds. I keep at this goal, and I feel great about my success. I'm not in any hurry. I do go to a diet center and learn the things I need to do. I create a healthy lifestyle for myself.

Exercise is a major focus, and something I learn to enjoy over the years. I finally feel I am alive and well. Before I just got through my days, and now I am beginning to really live. I recognize the difference in how good life feels without the burden of the sadness.

My life just keeps getting better and better. Somewhere along the weight loss trail I run into an old friend of mine from childhood. We start to date. This gives me joy because I reconnect with many old friends through him. He is fun to be with. My new life up to this point has not provided many 'fun' activities in my daily routine, outside of the time spent with my children.

All through the year I keep training my sales team, and I bring good information to the weekly sales meetings. I take this part of my job very seriously, and intend to make these meetings productive. I see my value as a motivator, but my intention is to be able to inspire. I keep a strong focus on this part of my job. Every Saturday morning at the sales meeting my enthusiasm vibrates the crowd. Wake up! Get excited! This is your life! Don't wait to be invited! No one is able to sleep at my meetings, and I have fun while delivering the chosen message.

Another challenge for all of us in the dealership, but especially the sales team, is that Volkswagen and Dodge both have product issues the last quarter of 1995 affecting not only sales, but the service and parts department also. Dodge has a major strike at one of its manufacturing plants which halts the production of most cars, and Volkswagen has cars with recalls on the steering wheels that contain the air-bags on our biggest seller, the Jetta. Volkswagen Jetta's are on hold at the port for months. The selling shelf is slim pickings for the sales team. We have very few cars to sell. This dry spell causes many salespeople to quit.

I see the walk-out coming, but am not in a position to take action. The only thing that will prevent the sales team from leaving is to pay a salary to keep them afloat. The owners are struggling as well, and are not willing to act with cash handouts. In January, 1996, all members of my sales team quit except the young woman who became my friend. When the sales team receives their quarterly bonus checks from Volkswagen of America the first week of January, out the door they go.

Now, I must hire and train a new team a.s.a.p. This is where my career really takes off. The pressure is on, and I need to rise to the challenge. The situation for me is "sink or swim," and it is a good thing I know how to swim. I hire and train five people immediately. By March we are in great shape. I discover that I am an excellent trainer. I love it! I love to teach others what experience has taught me. I use the weekly sales meeting to motivate and review the past week in a positive way.

My intention is to turn on the light inside of this new team, so they may become inspired and get out of their comfort zones. I always try to inspire my team to become better people. Motivation comes from an outside source while inspiration comes from within. With my happiness and enthusiasm I am a natural motivator. I constantly ask the team the same questions I once asked myself. Then something happens. The team becomes inspired. This makes me even happier, if that is even possible.

Business is on the rise. The Dodge franchise is gone by mid-year. Getting rid of Dodge is the best thing that could have happened for us at the time, especially for me. With the money from the new partner and the elimination of the Dodge franchise, the Volkswagen brand receives a new showroom. We move in during the summer months of 1996. We now have a beautiful, private facility. A new, fresh showroom only adds more excitement to the mix of this newly inspired team.

By the end of the year, the sales force and I finish top in our Market, the first time this store has ever even been close to the top spot. To reach the number one spot took a lot of hard work from everyone, but the result exhilarates us. I not only win a vacation to a beautiful resort, I also earn an extra $2,000.00 on top of my normal pay.

The Volkswagen rep had a $1,000.00 bonus on the table for me if I were to reach the top spot in his Market. When the owner hears of this little side bet, he decides to match the offer. They both thought the carrot was out of reach. The money is not what drove me, but the extra cash does add more fun to the mix. The excitement in the store the last month of the year penetrates to all departments, because as the saying goes: Sales drives the train. Everyone in the dealership is having more fun, but my spirits are over the top.

I buy my first house in 1996, a fabulous townhouse in a wooded area. Danny and I just love it. Jerome also comes to live with us a few years later. The circumstance that brings Jerome home to me is not a happy situation, but we all find comfort in being together. My gratitude really explodes.

I begin to reflect on my horrible life just ten years earlier. I can barely comprehend how fabulous my life is now having Danny with me. The joy in living with Danny, I have no words for. Plus, a beautiful home, a job I love, fun in a relationship, a free car with gas, free health insurance, so many free trips; my life is extremely fantastic. My reality is better than any dream I ever imagined. Never did I see all this coming my way.

In less than ten years I go from a life of sadness and living on welfare to this wonderful life. My earnings significantly increase every year but to see my son daily tops all else. My sons are the best gift God has given me in this life. I have found nothing that can compare.

I don't take any of my life blessings for granted. I give thanks every day for this life I have. I see my current situation as a miracle. Even today when I reflect on my life, all I see are miracles now. This is not the miracle I mentioned earlier. I have a way to go before I get to that one. But my life in 1996 does count in my book as a miracle. From the depths of where I came, to this fabulous life. I did survive, and I am alive.

Once again, I know I did not accomplish this success and find such joy alone. As I reflect on my past I become overwhelmed with gratitude that I did choose to be happy every day, and live the life I had to the best of my ability, because I now have such a grand life to share with Jerome and Dan. Where would I be today had I not?

Just when I believe life cannot get any better, I receive a pleasant surprise. Please come along with me to see how I receive the opportunity of a lifetime.

Happiness

Happiness is a means of transportation
Happiness is never the final destination
Happiness is the ride that carries you far
Happiness is the way; happiness is your car

North, South, East, or West
Does not matter, there is no test
Follow the lead, and plant your seed
Let go of all negatives; let go of all greed

So climb aboard and turn the key
Happiness is here, now, for you and me
Set a destination to receive instructions
Then get yourself moving in that direction

Christmas 1998 left: Jerome, Terri, Dan

It is not how much we have, but how much we enjoy that makes happiness.

-C.H. Spurgeon

Chapter VII

Changing Tides

The year is now 1997. Both owners invite me to move to the BMW Sales Management position. "We want you to do the same job you did for Volkswagen. We never saw anyone train a team as well as you did," they say to me. Both owners give me full rein to hire or fire anyone I choose, and I am able to set up the department however I see fit. How exciting! I never even thought of this possibility. I was so busy being happy right where I was in Volkswagen, BMW never entered my mind. I just did the job in front of me to the best of my ability.

I love every minute of this new, huge challenge. This new position is a real step up. In the automotive industry, jobs do not get much better than BMW Sales Manager, especially being given a free hand to create a new team along with the power to do as I see fit. My new position is bittersweet though, to leave my newly developed team behind hurts. I had put all my energy into developing this team. However, I know this new position is an opportunity of a lifetime.

In January, 1997, I take over as BMW Sales Manager. I hire three people immediately to make five sales people in total. These new hires really work out well and stay with me for years. Many become good friends. Enthusiasm and optimism are my natural state now, and I wake up each morning raring to go.

This new position brings different challenges, and I have much to learn. Once again, I receive no training. I need to figure things out on my own. With my previous position, the cars were on ground, ready to sell. The BMW brand at this time is very different. There are only a few cars on ground; most vehicles are ordered, and it appears there are not enough ordering slots for the demand. The shortage of availability creates very real challenges, and I need to learn fast.

The first mistake is our best teacher. The first ordered car arrives in March. The customer has been waiting since December for his new car. The salesman reports to me the car is here, but there is a big problem. The car has an automatic transmission when the customer ordered manual. We check the order. Sure enough, it's our mistake. This is a major issue. The manual transmission cars are not plentiful, but that is what the customer ordered. I do a search on the locator to see if there happens to be a vehicle that is a match to the original order. This will be a miracle if there is a match. It's a good thing I believe in miracles! On the locator I discover there is only one perfect match in the country. The vehicle is located a few states away.

Now, the question remains, will the other dealer surrender the car? I have no contacts or relationships at this point in my new career, but I can at least make the call to ask. When I explain the situation to the other manager, he lets me buy the car from him. He takes our car with the automatic transmission back in trade. I get a truck out to pick up the vehicle immediately, a brand new 1997 BMW 540i manual transmission. Our customer never knew the difference. This is one mistake that will not happen again on my watch. I count my blessings, and thank God.

The entire first year with BMW is very exciting to me. In February, I am still able to take the trip I won from my Volkswagen Sales Manager's position. A trip to Captiva Island in Florida, Viva! Captiva! A fabulous time with great fun, and I get a chance to say good-bye to many friends I made with Volkswagen over the last few years.

Back at work soon after my trip to Captiva, BMW announces a quarterly contest based on BMW 7 series sales, and the winners go to London for a week. I begin the same as I always do. I draw a picture of me hanging out of the window of the hotel saying, "Here I am!" With no clue as to what my odds are, I just do the best I can. If enthusiasm has anything to do with winning the contest, I will win. My energy is still skyrocketing, and I find it hard to believe how great my life has become.

Getting back to work after the week-long trip is actually fun. I love my job. The people I work with are super. The customers are wonderful. Many of these people have become friends over the years. How did my life get this good? These borrowed wings are really flying now.

Evidently some rain must fall. By the fall of 1997 I have a break-up with my old friend. The break-up takes me by surprise. I didn't think this relationship would last forever, but I'm just not ready to let go of the fun just yet. The fun we shared together really enhanced my time off and was a refreshing break from my long hours of work. The jolt of the break-up does wake me up to the fact I need to put more energy into my personal life. I have to create some sort of a fun outlet. "What will happen to me if I lose my job?" I ask myself. "I'll be lost." So I make finding a fun outlet a priority in my life to create a better balance. I need a hobby to get me out to meet new people, a social outlet.

I start to take partner dancing lessons. Dance has given me so much pleasure in the past, and I seem to have left dance behind when I began my new life. Partner dancing is a new challenge for me and appears to be a lot of fun. Dance adds a whole new side to life for me. I immediately am addicted. Dancing gives me a morale boost, plus fills the social gap for me, as well as helps to shed the last, few unwanted pounds; The perfect solution for many reasons.

At the end of my break-up I receive another Godsend. Due to illness the owner is unable to go to Europe to pick up a new car he ordered. Since I am his Sales Manager, I am the one that will go in his place. I get another free trip to Germany and can take a friend. Off I go and to drive his new BMW 540i stick-shift on the Autobahn and all through Germany for a week. The owner picks up the tab. How sweet can my life get? This is my first of many trips abroad. To drive the Autobahn is a great experience. BMW's are designed to drive that highway. I have a photo of the odometer at 140 mph. I had my friend take a picture so I could remember that experience and prove that I did reach that speed. What pure joy! Munich is full of so much life. One of my favorite places I find at the Neuschwanstein Castle in Fussen, Germany; Just positively outstanding. This trip is a fabulous bonus given to me. And the timing after my break-up is just perfect.

Getting back to business, the sales volume for BMW doubles my first year as BMW Sales Manager. Needless to say the owners are thrilled with my success. The store goes from 200 new units to 400. This experience is as much fun as I can imagine with work being involved. The hours are very long, nights and weekends, but I have the time of my life.

Before long the new partner takes over the entire operation. With the exit of the previous owner, BMW insists a General Manager with BMW experience is required before the sale can be approved. Here enters another change. I am not sure what to expect, so I just keep doing what I always do the best I can.

The new General Manager arrives in late spring. He has been with BMW for many years, but this is his first position as a General Manager. He is very personable and friendly but seems strict and inflexible in his policy. Within a very short period he fires my friend, the BMW used car manager, who is the person responsible for my being in management. This action is difficult for me, because I know he put his heart into this business, just as I do.

Not long after my friend is fired, the Volkswagen manager is fired, also. Another replacement is brought in. I am starting to wonder if I am safe, but I come to realize what will be, will be. To worry about my job will not help. I know for sure that worry is a misuse of my imagination. I can only do the best I can and hope for the best. So, I continue to do all I can do and enjoy this job I love. I am really in the flow now and have a good feel for the business. I have made many, strong contacts. In this position with so few cars, to have solid contacts is a big asset in making dealer trades.

I do win the trip to London to boot. My second trip to Europe comes in 1998. The trip to London is my first actual BMW trip, and gives me an added bonus. I invite my very dear friend, Lyn, to go with me. We have been good friends since first grade. Over the past ten years we haven't spent much time together due to life circumstances. With the hours I work, and she being a working mom with teenagers at home, time together has not been frequent. This trip gives us a chance to connect again. I just love sharing this experience with her.

On this trip I meet many new people and make some wonderful friends along with many, good business connections. One funny experience this group shares happens while posing for a group picture at Windsor Castle. The photographer, one of our group members, backs up slowly to try to get the whole group in frame. She continues to edge herself very slowly, backwards; before any of us realize, her rear foot steps back over the 'white line,' where the queen's guards stand for her protection. The photographer's foot motion is absolutely an innocent move. The guard shouts so loudly, "GET OFF THE WHITE LINE!" that everyone in our group jumps. This moment is sealed in our memories. Needless to say the photo was never taken.

Back to work, and the end of the year comes. The sales are at an incredible percentage higher than last year's 100% increase. Even with my success, when my time for review arrives with my new boss, I am still nervous. I'm not sure what to expect. I tell my boss, "I realize I'm the last manager standing since you came on board." He laughs and tells me not to worry. He proceeds to knock me over with praise. I am blown away. He's very hard to read, and his praise surprises me. This is a happy turn of events. I'm not to lose my job. My gratitude soars, and I am so pleased I did not waste any time with worry.

This was my first performance review, ever. The praise pushes me to do even better. After a few months go by, a light goes on in my head. I march right into the General Manager's office and say, "That's a dirty trick you pulled!" My boss looks at me puzzled. I tell him, "Ever since you gave me that great review, I've been killing myself to live up to it!" We both have a good laugh. He says, "Terri, you're doing great! Keep up the good work."

He taught me a great lesson with that review. Praise goes much further than criticism. I really did put more pressure on myself to do better after his praise. If he'd been critical, I may not have responded as well. So, I take this lesson with me as I manage others.

In March the BMW awards for the previous year are announced. I win the top prize, the BMW Grand Travel Award. I receive a week-long trip to Europe! This is such an honor for me and the dealership. This award is limited to a small percentage of managers. I'm now going to Barcelona, Spain and Munich, Germany! Oh, what a wonderful life. Gratitude pours out of me. My excitement is beyond words.

Sales keep growing. The rate of growth we have at the store is outrageous. The sales team keeps expanding also, up to seven, then eight. Demands on my time increase. My job is at a constant pace. The BMW manufacturer has its representatives stop in often. The two reps over the last few years both commented to me about the positive energy they feel when they walk in the door. Unlike many dealers they visit, this whole showroom buzzes with a good feel. Both reps credit me for this positivity. I'm happy to hear this news. I do my best to be as positive an influence as I can. I feel great that my efforts show.

Also, I create a system to measure floor traffic along with sales results. I need to keep track to see how many customers walk in, how many buy, how many come back a second time, how many take test-drives etc. I also track closing percentages for my team. Today, computers track all these facts. I do not have that luxury at this time. When my BMW rep spots my system, she asks if I will send the results to the main office weekly. I do just that. This becomes a standard procedure for years before the computer takes over.

To pay attention to detail is the key in management. My system allows me to see at a glance when the top sales people aren't taking enough new customers. It never fails that the top guns are busier than the rookies. The rookies have more time and talk to more customers, but the top guns have a better closing ratio. I need to make sure the top guns get in front of as many customers as possible. The store will do better. To correct this is not an easy task at my hectic pace, and my system helps me get a quick overview so I can do my best to push the top-guns in front of new customers.

On a personal note, this year I take my first cruise. I go with some of my new dance friends. The cruise is a 'Hustle Cruise' and I have a blast. Working weekends, I miss out on all of the dance events around the country that occur on a monthly basis. This cruise helps me make up for that. I meet many fun people, and dance my a** off, literally.

The following year, business grows, and I win the Grand Travel Award, again. This time the award is a trip to Switzerland. Winners get to drive brand new 3 series convertibles from Switzerland, through Austria, into Germany. I am also elected to Professional Sales Council. To earn council is a huge honor and gives me two shorter trips that are part business, plus a lot of fun. My life is so exciting and different from the sad days of my past. My goal to travel is more than I could ever have imagined with so many trips for free.

To win the BMW Grand Travel Award is no easy task. Many performance items are measured to even qualify, such as, growth, customer satisfaction, employee turnover, to name a few. I do work very hard. However, I know many people that work very hard at other centers that have yet to attain this achievement. I know my prayers help me achieve all I have. I am so grateful. My success is hard for me to believe. I've done so well, and I know for sure, I didn't do it alone.

I recognize that I have so much today, but my joy is not in the material possessions I have gained; my joy comes from having a home with my sons. Jerome is now living with Danny and I, and I enjoy every second of my time with them. The words are not enough to describe the feeling I wake up with daily. My day begins with me on the treadmill at 6:30 am while Jerome sits at the computer and makes funny gestures to mimic my motions. The memory of this simple gesture brings tears to my eyes as I write this. These are the moments I missed during the sadness and the memories I cherish today.

About this time I start to search for a deeper meaning to my life. I have achieved so much, but where do I set my next goal? I realize that I need a goal in order to get directions. Then, I receive a book as a gift, Conversations with God by Neale Donald Walsh. In this book the author asks God questions. God speaks through the author and gives answers. The book is a true conversation, a dialogue. This book reminds me of the dialogue I used to have with God as a child. With getting older and being so busy I still pray and get answers, but the conversation does not flow as it once did. I think I should make it a goal to get back to having a conversation with God.

There are many things God speaks of in this book. One thing that stands out to me is what God suggests we do when we face a decision. God suggests we ask the question, "What would love do?" and then make our decision. I can only imagine how much better this world will be if we all asked this question first. I love it. The book also starts me thinking about limiting beliefs. I realize I must believe 'that I have to work hard for money,' because I am at this point. I still love my job and I'm thrilled with the money, but I am working very hard. I have never been a fan of the long hours the car business demands. I saw the benefit to keeping me busy in those early, sad years, but I've never enjoyed spending so much time at work.

I understand beliefs and just what they do, but I don't know how to change mine, and I don't have the time to find out how to change them at this juncture. Too bad, I may have discovered my miracle fifteen years sooner. This book also leads to soul searching and cleaning my inner house, taking care of old business. I find a workbook related to this book and find several exercises to do. I learn how to get rid of my personal garbage.

Think about how many times a day or week we take out the home garbage. How often do we take our personal garbage out? I work on some anger issues, forgiveness, guilt, and other negatives, all the things that hold me back from the clarity I had as a child. Taking care of unfinished business allows me to live more clearly today. The weight of today is much lighter when I let go of yesterday.

This author has several books in this series. Over the next several years I read them all. God answers any and all questions in a brilliant manner. Of course! What else would you expect? A few books I need to read more than once. I am awakened to a deeper spiritual call. Here is where I set my new goal. My new goal is to go as far as I can in understanding God and this world we live in. God has done so much for me and given me this fantastic life, I intend to get as close to Her as humanly possible. Why does God have to be HIM?

For now, my career keeps moving up the ladder of success. I'm as happy as can be. My sons are with me. I have a beautiful home. Not only do I reach my goal of travel, I am traveling the world for free. Free is the most spectacular way to travel, with real red carpet treatment. I am so happy and grateful for these wonderful experiences.

I take my sons on a great vacation, another big blessing. I offer them a trip wherever they want to go in the United States. Off we go to California. We spend a week in LA, and take several day trips. We are all filled with pure joy. The only sad note: Jerome had just fallen in love with his future wife, Theresa, shortly before we left. He misses her quite a bit. Our trip is only a week, but to new love, a week feels like an eternity.

While on my European adventure in Switzerland, I meet many people. One person offers me a position as a manager in his store. He is the GM at one of the largest stores in the country. This offer is something to think about. I am honored. The position will require a move to Florida. When I tell my sons, they offer to move with me along with Jerome's fiancée Theresa, should I decide to go. My sons tell me that I have done so much for them that they will do this for me. Now my heart just melts.

I fly down to Florida for an interview. The BMW center is a beautiful, luxurious, state of the art facility. I get the royal treatment. All seems so glamorous. I have some thinking to do. When I talk the situation over with my son Dan he asks me, "What is the advantage of this new job?" I reply, "The position offers a lot more money." He gives me the best answer possible. He says, "Mom, you've never been about money." Here's the most beautiful answer I could receive. So we don't move to Florida, but we do make a move to a larger, more beautiful home nearby.

When I am ready for settlement, Divine intervention again assists me. I plan to buy the new house, and then settle on the old one the following week. I feel too overwhelmed to handle the move and two settlements in the one day I have off. I cannot take any more time off from work. Months earlier I had asked the General Manager if our 401K is set up to borrow from for a short term. He informed me it's not, and asks why. I explain I need $40,000 for settlement until I sell my house the following week. I respond that I'll just get a swing loan, no problem.

He speaks with the comptroller and gets back to me. He says that the company can swing me the money for a week. It's no big deal. This news makes my life much easier; at least this is how it appears to me at the time. The day before my settlement I go to collect the check. The General Manager is nervous. He apologizes. He says the owner is out of town and he can't get me the money. "What? Are you kidding me? My settlement is tomorrow! You offered me the money. It was your idea!" I said. Again, he apologizes. There is something he is not revealing to me, but the reason really doesn't matter to me. I said, "Last week when I reminded you about the money, all was good." He responds, "I know, I know! I am so sorry." Now I scramble as to what to do. It's ten in morning. I call my mortgage broker to see if we can reschedule the settlement. Not possible. The seller needs the sale for his new home purchase. I call my financial broker to see if I can borrow on my investments. He's in a meeting all morning.

While all this is happening, it's business as usual. Customers need to be handled. Salesmen need assistance. I'm not thinking clearly. I am panicked on the inside. By one o'clock there's still no response from my broker. I'm running out of time. I call my bank to see how fast a swing loan will take. No good. I need the money by tomorrow.

By two in the afternoon I still cannot get my broker. The banks will be closed soon. I call my sister Eileen to see if she knows the answer about borrowing from the broker. She uses the same broker. She tells me it's not possible to borrow on the investments. Now what? Eileen asks me why. I explain the situation. She tells me she just happens to be sitting on some cash. She took money out of one of her accounts and is deciding where to invest it. She has enough to cover me. Miracle? This news is certainly a miracle to me in the moment. Eileen tells me had I called later in the day or tomorrow, I'd have missed this opportunity. She transfers the money into my account. All ends well with another blessing from my family.

In December, 2000, I buy a bigger, more fabulous home with the most beautiful view. I look out my windows and just see rolling hills. It's spectacular. Jerome's fiancée Theresa moves in with us at this time, also. Jerome and Theresa marry in 2001 and stay on a year after that. I'm in my glory! My life is even better than any of my dreams. We are just one, big, happy family. My home is a peaceful haven for me to relax after the stress of work.

I feel I am on top of the world. My spiritual calling deepens, internally. Without enough knowledge of how to achieve my goal of going deeper within, I pray for direction.

Feeling Good

Feeling good is the key
Start now and you will see
Feeling good through and through
Unlocks the blocks that hinder you

Feel the peace
Feel the glee
Feel the happy
Let all else be

It does not matter what you do
As long as good feelings are inside of you
Just be in the moment, this moment now
Be happy and grateful, there is no how

Be in Spirit, inspired by Will
Be enthused, and keep internally still
Be kind and gentle so love will bloom
Remember...choose joy, let go of all gloom

Jerome and Theresa's Wedding 12/07/2001
left: Dan, Theresa, Jerome, Terri

You get the best out of others when you give the best of yourself.

-Edge Learning Institute

Chapter VIII

The Revolving Door

After Jerome and Theresa's wedding in December, 2001, the end of the year is very hectic at work. As I look back now, I can't remember a Christmas holiday I am not sick. The car business is always busiest at this time of year, and we usually lose our day off the last week of the year. With all the extra chores the holiday brings, I get run down and catch whatever germ is going around. Of course, this does not keep me from work. It just hinders my enthusiasm a bit and my time off a lot.

I feel better by the New Year. I'm in my glory. I am so happy with my entire life. It's the time of year for reflection and resolutions. I have a great life, what more do I need? I'm not sure how much more I can take on. I'm giving all I've got to this job. I love my work, but the job consumes so much time and requires so much energy.

I work-out on a regular basis. My dance life brings fun along with more exercise. I dance several nights a week during this period. I decide I need to read more. I enjoy reading; however, I don't do as much as I would like because I fall asleep at night before I can get three pages read. So this is my New Year resolution for this year. I begin to make time in the morning to read.

At this time there are nine salespeople on the team. My work is a constant stream of urgent matters to handle. The store has grown to about 800 new cars a year. The sales force has also grown, but not the management team. My workload is at the max. I love the challenge, but at times the team pays the price. When I am in a meeting for too long, the senior sales people have to fill the need, which only takes from their production. Unfortunately, I am unable to get this point across to my superiors. They think the bottom line will suffer if we hire another manager. I know we could increase production with a little more help. They feel I can handle the load alone.

My boss feels that the last week of the month all hands need to be on deck; no one gets to take their scheduled day off. I think this is asinine and tell him so. We argue behind closed doors, but at the end of the day, he is my superior, and I fulfill his wishes. Against my grain I make sure no one gets a day off the last week of every month. This includes me, and I hate it.

Golf is a big deal in the auto business, as in most businesses. The dealership sponsors a few tournaments every year. Several employees golf with our customers. My boss loves golf. This year the tournament happens to take place on the last day of May. May is one of our busiest months of the entire year. My boss is going to the golf tournament, plus four of my top salesmen. He enters my office just before he leaves to apologize. He asks me if I am angry he is taking away so many of my team. I reply "No, I am happy for you. I hope you have a great day. Enjoy. However, don't ever tell me I need to have all hands on deck for the end of the month again. I won't do it anymore." After this day, he never mentions it again.

The year continues, and the stress of my job increases. There are five steady salespeople, but the other four or five keep changing. To hire and train new people constantly puts a drain on my time. I love training new people when I have time, but my job has expanded to the point where I don't have a spare second.

As the end of the year gets close, I'm sick again, which is no surprise to me. This time I miss Christmas dinner. I do my best to stay healthy, but the job does take a toll. I'm still not able to convince my superiors to add some kind of help for the sales team. As long as I keep doing it all, they see no need.

The store finishes the year strong, but I do not win the Grand Travel Award, a trip to Australia. I am disappointed but can't complain. I have won more than my share. Besides the trip, the extra time off is what I value. The more time that goes by, the more trapped I feel in this job. The good news is how much money I make. Every year I earn considerably more.

In 2002 I now oversee eleven salespeople. My duties keep building, and the store continues in a positive direction. The store is managed with just little 'ole me running the entire sales department. This year brings added stress due to the introduction of a new BMW flagship car that has developed technical issues. The 2002 BMW 7 series creates a customer issue, and handling the unhappy customers falls on my plate. BMW steps up to back the product, and supports the Center's in doing the right thing to satisfy the customer. My job is to find a solution that's acceptable. This task is time consuming and stressful.

Each customer issue generates several hours work. Each case is different and requires its own solution. This added stress exhausts me. Also, at this point, the environment in the store begins to shift. The problem begins with my boss, the General Manager. He is the first GM the store has ever seen. He has done a great job, but something is happening behind his back. He uses me as a sounding board. Every time he's away for a day, something underhanded happens. He feels he's being set up.

Every now and again he shuts my office door and vents his anger. He's outraged that someone is filling the owner's head with bad ideas about him. He thinks it may be the comptroller that is the guilty party. I tell him to watch out for his friend, the parts and service director that he brought with him when he took the position. They are best friends. The General Manager tells me, "NO! He is my best friend, and he would never go behind my back." I tell him again, watch out for him.

In the meantime, the comptroller quits. She sees that the work environment is heading downward and makes her exit. She's the smartest one of all. After she leaves, the General Manager now sees that the backstabbing is still very apparent. He trusts me, and this is the reason he vents to me. He knows I'm too busy to think about anything else, and that is the truth. I appreciate his trust, but all of his outbursts only hinder my time. I have too much to do, always.

This situation percolates for months. As the year passes, things for the General Manager get worse. Finally, the owner enters my office, and proceeds to tell me I am no longer to report to the GM. I am to report to the GM's best friend, my new boss. I look at the owner in shock. "Does the GM know this?" I ask. The owner says, "Not yet, but he will."

What's happening behind the scenes is the purchase of another BMW dealership, located close to our center, and also a MINI store at a separate location. No one can talk about the purchase for legal reasons. Finally, after several months, my current boss is assigned as General Sales Manager and will be working in all stores, but not much changes immediately because the papers for the new store have not been signed. The new General Manager barely knows me and knows nothing about sales. He is no help to me in my busy state. I can really use some help on the sales floor.

As the year finishes, I wonder how we did so well. I have another banner year. I end up winning the Grand Travel Award once again. This year's award is a riverboat ride on the Danube, starting in

Budapest, Hungary. I am also elected to Professional Sales Council, again. This privileged honor totally amazes me. Even amid all the chaos, I succeed. I am so very grateful for this award and the extra time off that the awards bring.

2003 arrives, and marks the exact point where the job I love begins to fade. With the opening of the new BMW and MIMI stores, the chaos increases. The new stores are located about fifteen miles away. This BMW center is a bit larger in volume, especially in pre-owned cars, mainly due to a location closer to Philadelphia. My new boss is the General Manager for all stores. My old boss is the General Sales Manager for all stores, but mainly stays at the new BMW store which is located only blocks away from the MINI store. He harbors bad feelings towards the owner and the new GM, who mainly stay put at my location. Seems to me they are trying to bully the old GM out the revolving door. The service and parts director from the new BMW store now takes over that job for all stores. All the 'brass hats' are now working a triple load, which to me is not good business, but no one asked for my opinion.

A few positive things come from this purchase. My center now begins to close at 8:00 pm instead of 9:00 pm, to match the time the new BMW store closes. This extra hour does not sound like much but truly makes a huge difference in my life. Another positive for me is that the new General Manager sees that the other BMW center has more help than I do and that their managers make more money. I get a raise, along with a sales helper, someone to assist with some paperwork for me and the sales team. This is a very good day.

On a personal note, I receive a blessing in the form of what I consider an angel in my life. During the first week in January, 2003, I meet a young man while out dancing. He appears to have walked straight out of my dreams. He's tall, dark, and very handsome. He's also sweet and charming while possessing the spirit of a child. He's very playful. However, he's also much younger than I. He's closer to my sons' ages than mine. He invites me out. He's mature for his age, has traveled the world, speaks five languages, and is a genuinely, nice person. We talk about how our dating might work. What do we want from this? What are the expectations? He wants to keep it light. He's not sure how long he will be in this country. I tell him as long as I feel we are getting closer each time we are together, I'm happy. I'm not looking for marriage. Friendship is very important to me. We decide to give it a try.

I call him an angel in my life because that is how he appears to me. Right as the stress on my job is building, God puts this man in my life. We spend our time together with interesting talk and laughter, and he is a great diversion for me from the stress of my job. Whenever we are together, the time we spend is a pleasant exchange. We share our own little world where we participate in much 'happy talk.'

One day soon after we meet I see the Oprah show. This particular show just happens to be about women dating younger men, and how this is a good, new trend in the world. I have a good laugh, and feel a bit more comfortable about my new friendship. Another message from the Universe! I love when things like this happen. Another funny message comes to me the same way. I see Ivanna Trump in a TV interview. She is dating a man much younger in age. When she is asked about dating a younger man she replies, "I'd rather be a babysitter than a nurse maid." I love her answer, and feel very comfortable now.

With the extra hour off at work every evening, a few of my sales team and I join a local gym. We all appreciate this extra hour and are determined to use this time wisely. A few of us go to the gym together a few nights a week. So, in many ways my life is looking brighter. Exercise does help relieve the added stress.

In June I go on to the Professional Sales Council Meeting. This trip is a wonderful experience, and I see some old friends. We get the royal treatment. We have business meetings in the morning, and play for the rest of the glorious days. This experience is such a wonderful treat, and I leave feeling fantastic after my final day at the spa.

What I find back at work disgusts me. My sales team was rearranged without my knowledge. My finance manager now runs the MINI store, a big promotion for her. I am pleased and excited for her, but I am upset and angry that she is being replaced by one of my salesmen without any input from me. Now, I have an inexperienced finance manager who makes decisions in my absence, not to mention I now have to replace a seasoned salesman.

The big problem for me the day I return from my Council Meeting is that the managers from all three stores are leaving for "The Greenbriar," a resort in Virginia. The owner is taking the entire management team from all his stores so we can get acquainted. My boss, the General Manager, who made these changes without my knowledge is not in the store when I arrive. He went ahead to the resort to set up the arrangements for the weekend. I have no chance to speak with him about the changes. My anger just has to hold until this weekend is over. After the royal treatment I just received at the BMW meeting, the disrespect I feel stings.

Off I go on a six-hour road trip with the F&I manager that just left my team. She is very happy and excited for her promotion. She explains how the change happened really fast. The MINI store needed a manager on paper in order for the deal to clear. I understand how things happen, but as managers in the company, we all need to have our cell phone glued to our hip, and I feel disrespected for not being informed as to what was happening in my absence. She agrees, but is still very excited, and I am happy for her. She is a hard worker and deserves this promotion. We manage to have great fun on the ride to the resort in a BMW convertible with the top down, getting many honks from the truck drivers we pass on the highway and listening to great music along the way.

Upon arrival at the resort I review the itinerary for the weekend. The program includes dinner tonight and a meeting tomorrow and a list of all the speakers. Here's another kick in my butt. There's a whole page write-up on the new Sales Manager that was hired for the other BMW center, but who decided not to take the job. However, in the brochure is a welcome to him listing his accomplishments with BMW; the brochure also announces a floor time for him to speak at the meeting. My name isn't even mentioned, even though my accomplishments with BMW are equal to, if not better, than his. Reading the program just adds fuel to my already blazing fire. I am really angry now. Anger is one emotion I don't handle well unless I can address and release it. I will address the situation with the General Manager, but I will have to wait until Monday. This event isn't the proper venue for me to say anything. This is only Thursday. How do I get through the next few days?

At cocktail time, I go down to join the party. My old boss, my first General Manager, comes over to say hello, and he knows me very well and can see something is wrong. I explain the situation. He understands my position. I tell him I will address it on Monday, but I'm really fuming now. He rants on to say how this should not have happened and that it is a terrible oversight. The new GM has no idea what an asset I am to the company. He tells me both the owner and the new GM have no clue about the achievements I've made. They have no idea what an honor it is to win so many top awards. He tries to cheer me. He does make me feel better because I know he is sincere and has always had my back.

At the meeting the next day my old boss takes the floor, he goes on for half an hour on my accomplishments and the fantastic job I have done. I know he did this for me to help the owners and the new GM see my value. The truth is the hierarchy has no clue as to my value and accomplishments. My old boss knows the great job I do, and he appreciates me. I thank him. I'm not sure his attempt did any good for me, and I am quite sure it did not earn him any points. I do appreciate his effort. I feel better knowing someone cares.

Monday morning I have a talk with the new General Manager. He apologizes to me and acknowledges my feelings. He hears me out, and promises that any decision concerning my team will not be made without my knowledge in the future. He explains that everything happened so fast he did not have time to think. I at least feel better after we speak, even though nothing has changed.

Business slows down some in the last quarter of the year. This isn't good. This is the exact time BMW ramps up production on the 3 series which is the entry level vehicle, and the biggest seller. For years all BMW dealers screamed for more cars. We never had enough to fill the demand. In the fall of 2003, 3 series production is ramped up by about thirty percent. All of a sudden the demand drops for some reason. Now the BMW dealers have too many cars coming and not enough buyers. This turn of events appears to cause panic in the owners. The situation is not as bad as they perceive, but with two BMW centers in the mix, the owners have a large stake at risk. Here's where real chaos enters the picture.

Thank God for the angel in my life to counteract the chaos for me. He comes over one day and brings some pictures of his earlier days. There's a photo of him standing on a mountain. The grass is green with the sun shining. I get a flashback. I look at my friend and he's wearing a white linen shirt. His hair is long, dark and curly. I get chills. Twenty years ago when I was in the midst of my hell, my mother told me, "You are smart and beautiful. You can have any man you want." So, I looked through some magazines until I saw the right man. I cut out his picture and put it on a bulletin board. Every now and again I'd look at the picture and daydream about this man in my life.

The picture from that magazine is of a man with slim but muscular build. He is facing away looking over a grassy mountain, so his face cannot be seen. He's wearing a white linen shirt. His hair is long, dark and curly. The man sitting next to me looks just like that picture from long ago. The photos he is sharing with me remind me of that magazine photo. This angel is really right out of my dreams. If only I had saved that picture from an advertisement long ago. I share my tale with him, and we both enjoy a good laugh.

Another blessing amid the stress of my job comes in the fall; my trip down the Danube. I take along my friend Beth who's also in the BMW sales business. I met her years ago on one of my many business adventures. We became instant friends. We have a blast. A friend in the business really makes the trip fun because no matter how hard everyone tries to change the topic, the conversation always turns to the car business on these trips. Someone not in the business may not enjoy the conversations as much. Once again, I count my blessings for this beautiful life I enjoy today.

The year closes with a bang. The manufacturer places a great program to help move the stacking units and sales pick up. We are busier than ever, and this is good. Even mistakes go by without a fuss when things are busy. The owner only sees dollar signs. When things are slow, every little detail is picked apart.

The first big upset comes at the end of the year when the Sales Manager at the other store is fired after having a record breaking month. He is someone I know well. I have no idea why he's fired. Before the other store opened, the owner would always put me in the loop and ask my opinion, but not anymore.

Ever since the new General Manager took over, he makes sure he gets the only opinion in the owner's ear. The new GM is glued to the owner's side. He makes sure no one else speaks to the owner alone. This becomes a running joke with the employees, that if you see one of them, the other is very close. They are usually side-by-side. The employees tag them with the nickname 'butt-buddies.'

The revolving door of employee replacements begins turning faster now and affects both stores. With no rhyme or reason, all levels, all departments go round and round. And here begins the long trail of lawsuits one after another. The whole state of firing affairs seems a bit crazy to me, but again, no one asks my opinion.

The job of motivation which I love becomes harder for me now. I am determined to give all I've got to this team of mine because they deserve the best. We all work very hard. And my team needs my support. I put more steam in my engine and focus on bringing good vibrations into the atmosphere in the showroom.

By 2004, the stress level climbs even higher. Since my raise, I am making more money than ever. The sales team is at eleven people now, and my workload continues to expand. I love the challenge. I give all I can every day. Some days giving all I've got just doesn't cut it. There's always more work to be done, and some days the most important part of my job, supporting my team, takes a back seat.

In May of 2004 there is a Sales Manager's Conference. I head to Florida with over four hundred managers from around the country. I am one of only four female managers in attendance. I'm used to this fact by now in my career and feel grateful to be part of this group.

The first day of the conference marks another milestone for me in my life. The seminar is titled, "Yes, Attitude!" The program is facilitated by Jeffrey Gitomer, a sales guru and motivator, plus a real live-wire. He's also an author, and somewhat of a comic. This day is a full eight hours, and Jeffrey holds my attention throughout. I love this stuff.

Gitomer asks if we read or watch the news. Of course the answer is YES! I'm thinking this is what he's going for. He responds with, ***"STOP! STOP! STOP!"*** He continues on that the news is full of negatives. We need to fuel our lives with positives to gain a "YES, ATTITUDE!" He guarantees us we will still know what is going on in the world. We are told that in order to attain a "Yes! Attitude," we need to be in a positive state of mind and limit the amount of negative input.

My daily routine currently begins each morning with me on the treadmill watching the news. This is how I start my day. Also, the news is the last thing I watch at night. To stop watching the news sounds crazy to me. I'm not sure about this advice. The day continues, and he is a live wire filled with energy like I've never seen. His whole program is about getting to the positive side of life. I believe I do this already, but right now I need all the help I can get at the center to keep positive.

At this seminar we each receive a book and a CD to take with us. The book is The Five Major Pieces to the Life Puzzle by Jim Rohn. The CD is titled 'The Strangest Secret' by Earl Nightingale. The day has been very long. As the program ends and the managers exit the room, I hear many complaints. Many believe he's crazy about not watching the news, although everyone seems to be impressed by his attitude.

When I go back to my room to change for dinner, I find an invitation. I am invited to sit at the head table. At this table will be our top speaker for tomorrow's meeting. He is an auto designer for BMW. BMW's CEO will also be seated with us. There will be five other sales managers along with me. I am blown away. I feel so honored. The dinner is delightful, and our discussions go on until late in the evening. This is a night to remember.

The next day at the business meeting I'm still on cloud nine. The meeting is very exciting; we view the new car designs and learn future advertising plans along with the time frame for the ads to be shown. This is a good day, but I still hear many discussions about giving up the news. I'm not sure about this one myself.

On the plane ride home I read the book that was given to us at the seminar. This book is a short, easy read that's packed with great information. Mr. Rohn highlights many human behaviors and why we repeat habits that we know are bad for us. One point jumped out at me. The reason people repeat bad behavior is because they don't see the immediate results. Eating poorly takes many years before we get sick. Smoking takes a long time before we feel bad, etc. He illustrates the formula for success, that only a few positive, daily disciplines can offer immediate results. Start eating better and you feel better quickly. Start to exercise and you will have more energy almost instantly. I'm happy to see I practice what he proposes. He also says many habits are just as easy to do as not to do. For example, reading a book is easy to do, but just as easy not to. The result will not show up for years to come. This is why many people do not do the things needed to bring them more happiness. They do not know how certain actions will affect their lives.

After I finish reading Jim Rohn's book I make the commitment to stop watching the news. The thought of no news feels strange to me, but what do I have to lose? The environment at work is bad. If not watching the news can help my attitude, I am willing to try. The very next day I get on my treadmill and put on music instead of news. Immediately I feel more pleasure. The music motivates me to keep exercising longer. I like this change already. It is a great way to start the day. Many years later I don't miss the news. I probably heard of Michael Jackson's death a few seconds after you did, but I heard the news. I still know what's happening in the world. Now my focus is more in my world. I feel happier. I dare you to try it.

Next, I listen to Earl Nightingale's CD titled "The Strangest Secret" that was recorded in the fifties. Earl Nightingale is the father of self-help. He speaks of success and why one person succeeds and another fails even though they have the same education and aptitude. He states, "You are what you think about all day long." Mr. Nightingale speaks of how the mind is like a farmer's field. The soil doesn't care what you plant. The fertile soil of the mind will grow whatever seeds you plant, not caring if what you plant is good or bad. That's why it is important to be aware of what you think. Every thought is a seed that will grow with the right ingredients. He also mentions the importance of setting a destination in order to get direction. Otherwise, you just drift.

Jeffrey Gitomer, the facilitator from the "Yes! Attitude" seminar, made the suggestion of giving our sales team a positive feed every day. I start putting a positive saying on each desk in the morning. I like the response I receive. The store needs help with morale during this present chaotic time. The positive seed seems to help and gets people to talk about something positive. When I see this positive response, I take it a step further. After a few months I ask everyone to bring a positive thought to the Saturday meetings. My hope is that they will read many positive phrases to find one they like. At the meeting we all share positive thoughts. This works well for a long while.

By mid-year the new General Manager is gone. Just as he and I begin to meld his turn in the revolving door arrived. I'm not sure exactly what happened. All I know is he lost his 'family' status with the owners. This puts my old boss back in the saddle again, as General Manager, and this is a welcome change, but does not last very long.

A few months later another General Manager is introduced, and the original GM once again becomes the General Sales Manager for all three centers. The new GM is given a six month contract. He needs to turn business around in six months or out the door he will go. I am not sure what he can accomplish in six months but he seems smart enough to figure out what needs to be done. One good thing is he allows me to go to the BMW Manager's Academy, a program sponsored by BMW. This is something I've longed to do for many years but my old boss, for some reason, never allowed me to go. So I attend in the fall of 2004.

The first day at the Manager's Academy is spent mostly working a mathematical formula. This formula shows the expense of losing one employee. We work the formula on a ten-dollar an hour employee. This works out to be thousands of dollars. The lesson teaches us the value of keeping employees. My head begins to spin as I think of that old revolving door and the dollar signs attached to each spin. Not to mention the money lost in lawsuits.

At dinner the first evening I receive a call from my old General Manager and friend. He informs me that he has entered the revolving door. I can't believe it. This man is a valuable player, a real asset to the company. He gets tossed out for who knows what reason? I put his salary to the formula and my head spins again. This is just plain bad business in my opinion.

Things are now out of control. I give all I have to help my team. My enthusiasm is over the top. I know this because the new GM tells me, "Your enthusiasm is a bit over the top, don't you think?" In sales, you need to be upbeat and enthused to do well. My team needs to make a living. All employees are upset watching the revolving door and losing people they care about. Who's next? These actions diminish their confidence in selling when they're not sure if they will be here tomorrow. So I go over the top with exuberance to balance out the negative as best I can. A large part of my job is to motivate my team. I let them know how much I appreciate them and the job they do.

As the year closes, out goes the new General Manager. Even with a six-month contract he gets the boot after only three months. Round and round that door turns. Now, the current service and parts director becomes the newest GM. How long will he last? Some employees place their bets. He certainly is not a good pick for the position, in my opinion, because he has no sales background.

My co-worker, the used car manager, tells me this appointment does not bode well for us. The new GM was transferred from our other store and he has buddies he'd like to promote to take our positions. My co-worker is probably right, but I'll not even entertain this thought. "Hope for the best!" is all I say. I do not have the time for worry.

Mind over Matter

Mind over matter, a psychic sense?
Seems more a matter of common sense
To power your mind to control all you do
Mind over matter is not anything new

Christmas 2002 Jerome, Terri, Dan

Regard setbacks as opportunities to grow. Learn from them; research them; use them to propel you forward.

- Edge Learning Institute

Chapter IX

A New Road; the Journey Within

Back to where my story began. It's near the end of March, 2005 and the door is finally closed on the hot dog fiasco. Today is the Monday after the big sale. I'm called into the new GM's office. He tells me he doesn't know what's going on with the owners. "For some reason," he says, "there's nothing you can do right in their eyes." So, I ask him, "What do you mean?"

He tells me I have two months to get the new car sales up to 100 cars per month. (I have about a seventy-car average now) I say, "OK, what's the plan?" He says, "I don't think you understand. There is no plan. You need to get the store to 100 cars or you'll be replaced." Now, my ire is up. "Why don't you just fire me now? You know that it's impossible to just sell 100 cars magically. Even with a plan the job is nearly impossible!" I'm now very upset.

The GM says to me, "Don't worry about the gross profit; concentrate to get the units up. I'm fighting to keep you, but I can't understand why the Mr. is totally against you all of a sudden." I respond, "Is it because I did not take his side with 'M'?" He assured me that was not the case. "I had your back on that one. Actually everyone involved agreed with you. The Mr. actually agreed in the end."

My anger is coming to surface now, and I say, "There's the problem! You had my back in this situation because you were aware of what happened. The Mr. gets all sorts of negative blurbs about many decisions I make. To satisfy everyone is impossible! You are my boss and should have my back, but you have no idea about the job I do. You have no clue and therefore cannot back me."

The GM is now apologetic. He says, "I'm sorry. You're right. This is a new experience for me. I don't know much about the job you do, and have no time to figure it out." At least I get an honest answer. He tells me he'll talk to the owners. In the mean time I just need to do the best I can. He also tells me that two of the other managers I work with are not my friends, either. I know. They think if I am gone, they'll get my job. For years, many people have desired my position. I say, "Maybe that is part of the problem. Just know that whatever happens, I will not quit." "Good for you," he replied.

I remind the GM that I have scheduled some time off at the beginning of May. "Is it proper for me to take a vacation at this time?" I ask. He feels I should take it. "You need it more than ever now" he says. A vacation won't hurt your situation. Just do what you can." I leave his office frustrated, angry, and hurt. After ten years of hard work and dedication I am getting pushed out of my job for God only knows what reason. I really do not blame my boss. He has too much to handle and honestly does not have the time to fight my cause. I am just angry at the whole situation. To sell 100 cars is just about impossible to accomplish overnight. All I can do is the best I can. I inform my team of the situation. Most of them are upset and really do their best for me.

A few days go by, and the GM walks into my office, which is a rare occasion. He's usually never to be seen near the showroom, let alone in my office. He seems upset and tells me that one of my top salespeople is in the hot seat with the Mrs. He tells me the Mrs. wants him gone, and it is just a matter of time before she gets her way. "How do I reach my numbers if I lose him?" I ask. "I don't know, but he better look out. Also, the bear has to go," he tells me. "The bear," I say. "What's wrong with the bear?" In the showroom we have a large four-foot stuffed bear. He wears a company t-shirt and the children just love him. We prop the bear up in a convertible or on the hood of a car. He creates fun, especially for the children who visit. "Whatever!" I say. "The bear is gone."

I call the endangered salesman into my office to make him aware of the situation. He tells he knows why he's in the hot seat. He reports it's nothing to do with the Mrs., she and I get along just fine. "Really," I ask. The salesman says to me, "I guarantee this is a personal matter." I get the feeling he's probably right. I cannot imagine what the Mrs. may have against him. This salesman's sons visit the showroom often with their mom. They just love the bear. I tell him to watch his behavior because this situation is beyond me. I also tell him to take the bear home to his boys.

With all the stress and added pressure, I am amazed we ever sell a car. I do my best to put this situation out of my mind. There's nothing I can do about this problem. I know that whatever happens is meant to be. God always has a plan. I'm sure my thoughts sent a few prayers up 'to get me out of this mess.'

The last week of the month is super busy. The salesman in the hot seat has cross words with another employee, nothing big, but the GM gets wind of the fight. We finish with eighty new cars, and we are all happy for a very good month. Everyone gave their all, and I am grateful for the support I receive from my team.

I get called into the GM's office. He tells me that eighty cars is a good month, and he'll accept that. He also tells me I need to fire the salesman that is in the hot seat. He does not ask my opinion, and only one person is to be fired when there were two in the dispute. I'm so angry he hadn't asked my opinion. He just gave me an order. Also, I need to do the firing myself first thing Monday morning. The HR woman will not be in until noon, and this action cannot wait. This is absurd! He gives me no option.

On Monday morning I call the salesman into my office. He takes one look at me and says, "No problem, I'm leaving." He made my job easy, but I am still angry about how the whole situation played out. Thank God, I'm still good friends with him and his wife today. And thank God my vacation time is here.

Off to Mexico I go. I leave the next day to catch up with some friends who left a few days earlier. I'm so happy and grateful to have this week to chill. We rent a private home on the beach, a beautiful, spacious, fantastic home with a private pool, and a housekeeper. We each have a private bedroom and bath. There's a chef available also for our meals, if we desire.

In the middle of the week we decide to have a massage therapist come poolside, and we all take turns getting a relaxation massage. After my massage I get on a float in the pool. I'm just drifting on the water. With the heat of the sun on me, I melt into bliss. I can't tell you how long I'm there. I go into the silence of my mind and tune out the world. This is my first real experience with meditation. In the silence I hear nothing. I feel nothing but peace. I can't tell you if I am in that state for an hour or two, or if it is ten minutes. All I know is within the silence I feel God. I feel the peace and serenity within. I know that whatever happens in my life, I'm going to be all right.

This is just the vacation I needed, a real Godsend. Upon returning to work, I enter through the rear of the building. There are about twenty steps leading up to the back door. As I climb the stairs I can feel the stress building with each step I take. The tension in my shoulders and neck by the time I open the door is overwhelming to me. But, back to work I go.

The job is difficult knowing that whatever I do is futile. There's nothing I can do at this point to save my job. I need to put on a positive front for my team. They deserve to have the support they need. The pace is hectic the entire remainder of the month. May finish's with seventy cars. There's only so much my team can do. They all feel bad and I let them know how much I appreciate the fact that they care. By now, I know I'm getting fired. I will lose my job, but I'll be all right.

June begins and to my surprise I am still here. I keep waiting to see when my last day will happen. The owner hasn't spoken to me in months. This month I have a fundraiser that we sponsor every year. The event happens mid-month, and I'm still here. I put a great deal of effort into this event and bring in many outside vendors to donate their time to help the cause. We get a great turnout, and the event is a success.

In the middle of the event, the HR woman comes over to me and gives me a big hug. She tells me what great job I have done for this event. Our sister store had its event yesterday and was nothing to compare, she reports. As she's hugging me, she starts crying. I just look at her and tell her to just get it over with. I know I am getting the boot, and that knowledge makes my job even more difficult. A few days later I take my turn in the revolving door.

I do get a great severance package along with a convertible roadster to use for six weeks. This is quite unusual in the auto business. I am sad leaving the team I built. But, in reality the job I love has been gone for quite some time. I'm happy to get away from all the stress.

My replacement isn't the right man for the job. He is one of those 'big shot managers' I mentioned earlier. Good thing he did not last too long. His replacement is a good fit for my team, and surprise! he just happens to be best friends with the current GM. But he is a good fit, and that is what I care about.

The GM and the HR woman go through the revolving door within a year or so after I leave, and so does the personal secretary, 'the spy.' I believe I'm one of the few that did not sue. I am just not that interested in the fight. I actually love my life and count my blessings to have some time to unwind. The used car manager also gets a turn to spin in the door.

I receive a job offer immediately. The offer is a job I may have taken had it come at a later date. I'm determined to take the summer off to unwind. I need to relax and am set on doing just that. Months pass before I am able to totally relax; however, the tension and stress from the past few years finally fade. To walk away from a job I love makes me sad, but it seems easy in comparison to my past sadness. Actually, everything in my life seems easy to me compared to my past pain.

For the first time in my life I now have time to relax and money to spend. I enjoy this break immensely. I travel to South Beach with a friend and to the Jersey shore many times to hang with friends and family. I realize I enjoy not working. I also discover I love the Oprah Show. I've always liked it but only saw it here and there over the years. I enjoy her show so much I decide I need to purchase a Tivo before I go back to work. I need to keep up with Oprah. On one of her shows I hear Oprah mention one of her prayers. "Thank You for using me for something greater than myself." I immediately adopt this prayer and say it often.

One day online I come across a 'Happiness Survey'. It may have been on Oprah's website, I'm not sure. I know I'm happy so I decide to see how I do. The survey is filled with many questions. I answer each question honestly. After about forty or more questions I hit a roadblock. I stumble on the question, "Now that you know the outcome of your life, would you make the same decisions and choices?" This question takes me right back to my divorce, and the decision I made to walk away with nothing. I know this decision was Divinely guided. I only hope I would have courage enough to make the same choice. Fear comes over me. I go into a panic. I shut the computer off and just cry. I fear I'm not strong enough to walk into hell, knowingly. This question has me upset for days, and I never finished the survey.

Even though I make the most of my time off, I begin to get a little restless by late fall. As the cold weather sets in, available activities diminish. There are not as many fun things to do that keep me entertained. I actually have a few down days. Very unlike me and I snap out of the doldrums quickly. Faith, trust, and gratitude take over.

While I search for work, I fear I may never find a job I love again. I go to several interviews and even have a few offers. However, not one job appeals to me. I decide to wait until after the holidays to search again. As the end of the year approaches I feel my job is close. I just have a feeling. As the holidays arrive, I realize I am not sick as I'd been previous years from the job stress. I totally get to enjoy all aspects of the season with joy. This is so different for me. I'm very grateful to be in such good health. I get to enjoy Christmas, and have the time to relax. This holiday feels so different without the pressure of the job.

Finally, in January, my friend Beth calls to inform me of a BMW manager's position that opened. The dealership is about an hour's drive. I know the owner from many years in the business. Beth and I were with him on our trip to Hungary. I call him immediately and he say's "Terri, you're the first person I thought of. I was looking for your number."

On February 6, 2006 my new job begins. I'm so enthused it's hard to contain myself. I've known one member of the sales team for years, but all four salesmen make it an easy transition for me. One salesman starts the same day as I do, but the others have been there for quite some time. They are all seasoned and need little encouragement from me, a much different atmosphere from what I'm used to. My title here is Sales Manager. I'm considered a General Sales Manager with BMW due to the fact I handle new and pre-owned vehicles. I am the only manager outside of the owner. This is a much smaller store in size and units than my previous position.

I learn to handle the pre-owned side with ease. Even though I have a general understanding of the system, I've never actually done the work before. I learn quickly about appraising cars, re-conditioning them, certification and lease-end returns. There's a lot to learn, but I catch on fast.

The most disappointing of all to me is there are no sales meetings, ever. I called a meeting the first week. The owner looked at me as if I had twenty heads. He let me know that meetings aren't necessary. We are a small group. These men are seasoned pros and know what they are doing. This really hurts me because to me meetings are a good thing. The owner has had bad experiences where meetings became scolding sessions. My enthusiasm is ready to burst and I need to find an outlet.

This position is a huge step down from my previous position where I did so much at a hectic pace. Here, all runs at a much slower pace. To slow down, takes me months to adjust to, if not years. I keep hearing from the team, "You're not in Kansas anymore, Dorothy. Take it easy!" To slow down is a difficult task for me.

The income is a big adjustment also. I am making about forty-five percent less. The money is still good, and I'm very grateful to have this position. The bright side is that the hours are much less, even with an hour commute each way. I work from noon to seven-thirty every day but Saturday. Saturday hours are ten to four. I have

Wednesdays off. Another plus is there is no stress. The owner is a working owner and understands the business. He appreciates every little thing I do.

At this point I'm able to put more focus on my own life. What direction do I intend to go? How do I reach my goal of knowing God better? I start listening to audio books to enhance my long ride. Dr. Wayne Dyer's The Power of Intention, given to me as a gift, is easy to listen to. The audio book is filled with great information about how to enhance my life. One of my favorite messages is the image he presents from when he was a young child on a trolley with his mother. He tells us how life is like a trolley ride. People come into our lives and some ride for a while, and then get off. Others ride with us all the way through life. Some other people may get on, then leave, and may get back on again. All we need to do is to hang onto the trolley strap, and let the rest go. I love this concept! Seems to be a good way to let go of control, and I use this image many times if I feel the urge to resist something. Or, if I feel the need to take control of an issue I can't control. I think 'trolley strap!'

Dr. Dyer also speaks of 'thinking from the end,' that is to act as if you already have whatever it is you desire. This is difficult for me to grasp at first. Then I look back to the time I set the goal to be a manager. I realize that in playing my little games, thinking from the end is exactly what I had done. I had begun to think as a manager and looked at things just as I imagined a manager would. I did think from the end.

So now I'm in search of a future goal. Where do I want to go from here? A spiritual journey and what else? I use my morning hours the best way possible. I have an exercise routine that allows an hour and a half for exercise; I walk on my treadmill, stretch, jump on a small trampoline and lift some weights. I absolutely love my mornings off. I'm usually up before seven and need to leave the house by eleven. This allows plenty of time to fit in everything at a leisurely pace, a very different life style for me. I adjust easily and love the morning hours. I am so grateful to eliminate the stress from my life.

On the work front my enthusiasm just bubbles out of me. I start to celebrate every sale as I'm used to doing. I start woo-whoing all over the place. One day as the owner is on his way home, he calls me from his mobile phone. He says, "Terri, I just love the woo-whooing! Thank you." I certainly lightened the spirits in the place. Another bright note, due to the fact that the owner is hands-on, he's able to see the job I do. He is so appreciative of everything. He hears me on the phone with a customer and comes over to say, "Thank you, I like how you handled that." To be appreciated is a breath of fresh air to me.

During the spring of my first year there a customer comes in with a very new, very expensive sports car. His wife hates it and he needs to trade it in on a sedan. The vehicle is only about six weeks old with about 1200 miles on the odometer. The gentleman is shopping every dealer in a fifty-mile radius to cut his losses. The competition is fierce.

We have a BMW 750li that he likes but he'll not accept less than $100,000.00 for his trade. The most I am able to get locally is about nine thousand dollars short. This number is right in line with most of the dealers he shopped. I pick up the phone and start calling some contacts I have in California. The first few contacts do not pan out. The third person I call will pay me $100,000.00 for this car and cover the transit cost. We make the sale. WhoWhoo!!!

The owner is so impressed that I even thought to make that call. He asks me, "How did you even think of that?" I look at him and say, "It's my job to know." The California market is hot for this type of car. The value can be much greater there at times. I only call people I know and trust. The person who bought the vehicle has a customer searching for just this particular car. He's willing to pay top dollar for it, and we both make a sale.

This is where my experience and relationships are of great value. Outside of a few rare occasions like this, I feel my talent is not put to good use in this new position. This job does not provide me the challenge I love. This sales team is very independent. There are no customer complaints that occupied more than half my time before. However, I do love and value the extra time off that this position allows me.

For now I remain grateful. I love to feel appreciated on a daily basis and work in a no stress atmosphere. I focus on the positives of this job. The hours are fantastic. The atmosphere is wonderful. There's work to fill my day in a casual way. The people are fabulous.

In August, 2006 my family and I are devastated with the news of my sister's Kathleen's sudden death from a heart attack. She never regained consciousness after her initial attack. This is a shock to all who love her, and a very sad time for her devoted husband, her seven children, two grandchildren and her four sisters, and the many others who loved her. Did I mention earlier, that Kathleen left the convent three years after she entered? God held a different plan for her. She became a wonderful wife and mother. God bless you, Kathleen. We miss you.

I'm at work when I hear the news that my sister is unconscious. I am told the attack is believed to be a heart attack. I'm in shock with this news. She was traveling across country with her youngest daughter, visiting two of her other married children. I just had received an email from her that morning. We all did. She gave us an update on her oldest son's upcoming poker tournament

When I get home from work, there still is no more news. I kneel down and say the rosary. I feel anxious and it's difficult for me to just sit alone, so I decide to do what I normally do, dance. Tomorrow is my day off, and this is my usual dance night. In the middle of the evening I dance with a man named Angel. He's not a regular on the scene, but I know him. As we dance, I feel my sister pass through me. The thought I receive is 'I can see why you enjoy dancing so much.' Then she's gone.

I know in this moment she passed on. I have a sinking feeling. I am very grateful not to be alone. I think of her daughter far away and send her my love and prayers. I'm hoping she's not alone at this time. My sister's death jolts me into high gear about my own fitness. I research many health products and decide what my best course is. I get physically checked to make sure all is good where my health is concerned. I make the changes I feel are necessary.

Later in the year I enjoy one of the best blessings ever, one I will treasure forever. My sons and I take a Caribbean Cruise together. We join a group trip with many extended family members from my daughter-in-law Theresa's side. We have a fantastic time. All of us get the most pleasure and fun we possibly can. This vacation is one of those moments to just savor the joy. And I do just that. Just to write about this trip brings me joy.

I also savor the joy of each and every morning. My drive is very scenic with no traffic. I really delight in the beauty of all the seasons as the year goes by. One morning on my way into work I'm listening to some music. I'm in a glorious state enjoying the scenery as I approach the top of a hill. I can see the many rolling hills and mountains of the Reading, Pennsylvania area on a bright, sunny day.

As I approach the top of a hill I get a sensation in my body, along with the immediate thought that tells me I'm to write a book about my life. I'm happy for this information, and at the same time clueless. This info needs to sink in. How? How do I accomplish this task? I at least know now where to focus my future. But I have no idea how. I purchase a few workbooks. I do the work and ask myself the questions. I do some writing exercises. At this point, however, I'm not sure what part of my life I'm to write about.

I don't mention this new idea to anyone. With no clarity in my mind on how this book is to develop, I don't know what to say. Then, all of a sudden, when I am at home relaxed one afternoon, the title flows to me, it's Silent Dancer. I nearly fall off my feet. This information blows me backwards into a chair. I get the message. I now know exactly the part of my life I am to write about. I am to write about the section of my past, after divorce and before my new dream. This is the part of my life where I totally detach from my feelings before I spiral out of control.

So here is my new goal. My belief system at this time doesn't support the possibility of being without a job. I begin to write in my spare time. I dance all around my life story but when it comes to the sad part, I'm not able to get to the core. These feelings do not come out of me. On the other hand, I do start to mention my goal to a few people.

In 2007 I listen to many more audio books. Mike Dooley is an interesting fellow. His audio book Infinite Possibilities, The Art of Living Your Dream, gives me many hours of listening pleasure. His platform is "Thoughts become things, choose the good ones!" I begin to realize just how my thoughts do shape my world. He delivers a wonderful message in a delightful way.

Mike Dooley also sends out Note's from the Universe, which eventually becomes a book. These are just delightful emails five days a week. Once you fill the information in, and provide your goal, you start to receive his personalized notes. He speaks as the Universe, and is usually funny and thought provoking. Every once in a while I get an email that speaks of my best-selling book. This is a fun thought.

For the most part my thoughts serve me well. I realize the weight I intend to shed isn't dropping off because 'I think I need to lose weight.' I think I'm fat, so therefore, I am overweight. I decide right here and now, I will never think or say I'm fat again. The truth is: I'm not. I can go back through any photo in my past adult life and tell you how much I weigh in each picture. Most of them I am really thin. How ridiculous is that? I see myself looking fabulous in a photo. Then I recall how fat I thought I was and what I weighed at the time. I will stop this madness, now!

No more, I promise myself. At this time Rhonda Byrne produces The Secret DVD. I find this good information, and start to listen and read many of the teachers in the DVD. Most have audio books and I'm very thirsty for this knowledge. This subject fascinates me. I actually was into The Secret before Oprah did two shows about it. Imagine that, me ahead of Oprah. This is a first.

The Secret presents the law of attraction, how we create our own world with our thoughts and feelings. I look around and am very pleased with my world. However, if I'm able to create anything, I'd like to create a life with more freedom. No more being locked into a job that steals my life. Get rid of those limiting beliefs! I will figure out how, I promise myself.

I remember the picture I cut out of the magazine twenty years ago. My angel friend that I felt came out of my dream. Did I attract him to me from my daydreams? Did it take twenty years because my feelings were so detached? I remember the chill I got when I realized he was so similar to that picture from a magazine. This thought really makes me wonder. Is this how the law of attraction really works?

Speaking of my angel, he moved overseas this past July. I am sad to see him go. Neither of us can believe how fast four and a half years went by. We'll stay in touch. I feel blessed for the beautiful memories. Good-bye my friend. Thanks for the joy, and happy trails to you.

Another author to enlighten me is Eckhart Tolle. The book The Power of Now is packed with great information. The main message for me is that God exists in the 'Now.' Compare this to driving your car. If you are distracted by texting, you're not paying attention to the moment. Bad things can happen. In your life if you are not in the present moment, God cannot get through. You miss the signals from your surroundings. Now is the only moment that counts.

In his book A New Earth, Eckhart Tolle speaks of many things. So many that Oprah did an on-line course that went on for ten weeks if I remember correctly. And yes! I did them all. What stands out to me the most is just to enjoy all you do. A very simple message: Enjoy what is. But if reality is something that you can't enjoy, accept it. Lack of acceptance creates resistance. Resistance creates pain. How well do I know that lesson?

I laugh at some of my friends. I know someone who hates grocery shopping. Fiercely! She hates it. I can't imagine hating something I have to do all the time. I've always been fascinated with all the choices we have in the stores today. I must have a past life that had no luxuries. Another friend of mine hates cleaning. I have to admit when I worked so many hours I had help for cleaning. Now that I am off, I enjoy it. To clean house gives me instant gratification. I love my home and love it even more when it shines.

In A New Earth the author also tells a story that I love. He speaks of two monks on a journey, one elder and one young. They walk about eight hours to their destination. These monks are vowed to silence, and are to have no interaction with others. Early on in their journey there's a woman attempting to cross a muddy street. She has difficulty with her dress and struggles at the side of the road. As the monks get close to this woman, the elder monk lifts her and carries her across the muddy street, without a word being spoken. The two monks continue walking in silence. Many hours later as they approach the end of their journey, the young monk breaks his silence. "Why did you pick up that woman? You know we're…." The older monk cuts him off. He says," I put the woman down hours ago, why are you still carrying her?" I just love this story.

How many times do we carry something and keep it going around in our mind? Even the next day we pick it up again; especially if we feel wronged by someone. These are the things that block us and keep us from living in joy. Let go! Take the garbage out. Start the day fresh.

In January of 2008 one of my life long dreams is fulfilled. I've longed to go to Hawaii ever since I was a child. My sister Rosemary came back from her vacation there with fabulous photos and tales. I loved hearing about her travel there, and have always yearned to go. This is the year I'm able to cross this dream off my life list. Too bad this is not a free trip. Seriously, I'm very grateful I'm able to pay for it. My friend Pat asks me if I'd like to join her. This is a cruise sponsored by a dance studio in our area. This is a seven-day cruise and we'll stay a few extra nights before the cruise sails. It's all very exciting. My finances are tight due to making so much less over the last few years, but I cannot resist. Thank God I saved!

There's a whole group of people I know, and we have a blast. We do everything there is to do. The weather isn't as good as in my dream, but it is good enough. I'm so grateful this opportunity came to me. I count my blessings. In my travel time to Hawaii I read a small book by Deepak Chopra titled The Seven Spiritual Laws of Success. A very short, easy read, filled with potent information. The message resonates with me. I take action immediately. He strongly suggests meditation. I heed his advice.

My morning ritual now includes meditation. I feel some benefits right away but am not always able to quiet my mind. Sometimes I can, but many times not. I have the main focus of getting rid of these limiting beliefs. I keep searching for more information. There's one common theme from many sources I read. I need to change the programming in my mental computer.

The unconscious mind produces whatever is in the program. Our program doesn't care what it produces. Most of us are programmed at a very young age. So now I know what needs to be done. The question remains, how? Meditation is a good way if you can get to deeper levels. Affirmations help if you are really able to feel and believe the affirmation.

So, of course I pray and ask the question. "How do I change my program?" I'm now wondering why I didn't ask this question ten years ago. Ask and you will receive. God only knows where my life could be by now had I asked that question back in the nineties. The answer comes to me by way of email. I'm on the email list of many teachers from The Secret. In one of the emails is a message about a system of meditation that induces brain waves. With this system a deeper level is guaranteed. This system requires the discipline and commitment of an hour a day. I research the system and know it's the answer to my prayer. I make the commitment to myself to do this. I take the plunge.

I notice some changes right away. My dreams take me on a journey through my life. The dreams are not really very meaningful but give me an indicator of my path. I go through my whole life. Then I finally have a dream that is of the present day. I think I'm through all the thresholds of my mind. I'm not aware that this is where my deeper level begins.

With this system I also record, in my own voice, many affirmations on a disc. I listen to the disc while sleeping. The affirmations are superimposed on ocean sounds. Of course, one of my affirmations is that 'I let go of all limiting beliefs.' Meditation right away clears my mind of static. I see a clearer thought channel immediately. Meditating also gives me a deeper feeling of peace. From all I've read, feelings are the most important thing in creating life. When you feel good, good things happen. I say this quite a bit.

Just as exercise strengthens the body, meditation strengthens our connection to the power of our Soul. With physical exercise, when you first begin, you may feel some pain afterwards or have sore muscles, but with continued, routine exercise the soreness subsides, but you still feel the muscles for hours afterwards. The exercise brings an awareness of your body into your consciousness. With meditation, once one gets past the initial phase and learns to quiet the mind, awareness is gained, just as in physical exercise. Only this awareness is of the power we all have within and of the energy that connects us all. Our Soul is going to be here long after we are gone, and it only makes sense to tune-in to the power of the Soul while we are alive.

The way I see life, we are all cells of the same body. Each cell has its own function, and every cell is important. Whoever and whatever is here belongs in this world. In meditation, a connection with the source of power comes alive within and over time provides the clarity and the ability to see that we all are connected to the same power, which I call God. Our bodies keep producing new cells all the time as the old ones die off, and over time every cell gets replaced just as humans keep reproducing life on our planet, and eventually every person (or human cell) is replaced. So in my mind, to plug into the power within only makes sense. If everyone plugs into his or her own power, and that power connects us all, there will be a more coherent state on the planet with all living in peace for one power greater than each individual, everyone happy in his or her own purpose. Heaven? I believe we are closer than we think.

Each of us is like an electrical appliance that is useless when not connected to electrical power. But because we have free will to live as we choose, many are not connected to the power because they cannot see past the material world. Most people I know don't know the difference meditation, or being plugged in, will make in their lives, and therefore, don't make the time to discover this truth. So often I want to scream at the top of lungs! Wake up! Tune-in! I do understand the difference meditation makes.

So after my new daily routine every morning, my team at work gets an earful when I walk in the door. I'm in such a good mood. I feed myself positive information on my ride in. Positive is spewing from my pores by the time I arrive. I have fun with my enthusiasm. At least, I make my co-workers laugh. One thing I often say is "Good thing I'm thin and rich!" This is to counter all the years I used to say I'm fat, or I need more money. Many times I walk up to one of my sales team members and say, "Look! I think I look younger today, I'm really getting younger. What do you think?" I am a piece of work, and I love the fun I have.

With my morning ritual I start the day feeling so good. I begin to call this feeling 'inside the rainbow.' I feel so centered, peaceful and happy. I believe I get a glimpse of heaven. Unfortunately, the feeling fades by the end of the day. Every day I walk in the door at work filled with joy. The guys I work with are great, genuine, nice people. The customers are friendly also. The atmosphere is so relaxed. Customers stop in just for a cup of coffee or a chat. I call our work environment "Andy of Mayberry" because the atmosphere is so relaxed in comparison to where I worked previously.

One of the many positive feeds I use is a book called The Science of Success by James Arthur Ray. This book is another short book filled with great information. This book helps me develop my dream of writing by showing me some exercises on how to put a dream together. One thing James repeats in this book is: Energy flows where attention goes. This feeds right into why you are what you think. All thoughts are energy. This information all fits.

I find it sad that many people I know read book after book but never apply the information. Many people are unhappy yet unwilling to take action. Instead they complain about this or that. Complaining is such a colossal waste of time. I can't say I put into practice everything I read. I examine the information to see what is right for me. I do take action when something resonates with me. Once I decide on a certain course of action, I commit. I focus full force. Sometimes I go overboard and create resistance. I recently discovered some resistance I created and will tell you about that shortly. One thing for sure is that I put all of me into my life. I'm grateful I learned how to choose happiness. I see now how being optimistic and happy has shaped my entire life. Thanks again, mom.

In truth, if you do not put all you can into your life, you only cheat yourself. Nothing gained is a loss sustained. Only you are responsible to feed your mind, body, and soul. What are you waiting for? I believe most of us know what needs to be done. Some may not know what their passion is, but if you start to be happy right where you are, get yourself clear and look inside, you will discover your passion.

With the close of 2008 the BMW center where I work wins "The Center of Excellence Award." This is the highest honor a center can win. My boss is very grateful to me. The center has always had high scores but never enough volume in sales to win. This is a proud moment for all the employees. The owner and his wife get a great trip. The store gets bragging rights and a trophy. I am very happy for the owners and excited to be part of a winning team.

As 2009 rolls in, I'm not feeling as vibrant as usual. I notice my energy wanes faster than usual, and I fall asleep watching TV in the evening, which is not the norm for me. I feel something is not quite right. My intuition tells me this may be a thyroid problem. I go to my doctor for some blood work only to find I'm right. I have hypothyroidism. My doctor starts to write me a prescription. I tell her, "No. I don't want to start on medication." I know once I take the medicine, I may need it forever. She is shocked. She says there's not much I can do to fix my thyroid. This can be dangerous if I get farther off-count. I tell her I need to try. She says, "The possibility of a cure is really what you believe, but you need to promise to return in six months to be tested again." I agree to be come back then.

The first thing I do is go to my chiropractor, Dr. Brian Capaldi, at Peak Potential Wellness Center. I ask him about my spine. What controls the thyroid? He shows me and assures me this is not the area where I have issues. I ask him his opinion about healing my own thyroid. He feels I should give it a try before taking medication. He believes in holistic ways. Brian is the only person I know who encourages me on this healing path. Everyone else says I cannot heal my thyroid. I'm convinced I can do it. Many books I've read tell tales of such healings. The human body is a self-healing machine. You cut yourself, and with the right conditions your skin heals. I believe the whole body works this way. I need to find the right conditions to help my body heal. Of course, I pray for direction.

Next, I check online. There's no information about healing a thyroid. Funny, that today, only a few years later, there is lots of information and research on healing a thyroid. I look to see what a healthy thyroid looks like. I think about this picture during meditation. I give thanks for my good health.

A book about diet is suggested to me. I read and discover the healing power of fresh juice. I feel this is worth a try. I start juicing. In the morning fresh juice is all I have, eight to ten ounces of fresh squeezed juice. I have some more a half hour before lunch. The juice helps with digestion. I have salad and vegetables for lunch, only food that's easy to digest, a high-energy diet.

I do this routinely. With no food in the morning, and with the sugar from the juice, I'm flying high by the time I get to work. I'm really wound up with only good, positive feelings. I share my thoughts of the morning with all. Before I know it, I'm given the nickname 'Fortune Cookie.' All the positive sayings are naturally ingrained in me and I naturally respond with a positive quip to everything that crosses my path. The nickname Fortune Cookie ignites a passion in me instantly. I love it! Right away I begin sending daily emails to my co-workers with a positive thought just as I had done once before. Of course, I title the email "Today's Fortune Cookie." I add my children to the list. Eventually, I add some of my old sales team. Somehow this gesture isn't enough to satisfy my passion. I'm driven to do more. Feeling this passion makes me miss the days when I had a team to motivate, and a meeting to prepare and facilitate. I remember how I loved feeding positive information to my team. My message then was only absorbed by some, but the people I did reach let me know how grateful they were. I miss those days.

In the fall of 2009 I go to a business meeting. I run into a young gentleman from my old sales team whom I had hired and trained out of college. He sees me and lights up, gives me the biggest hug and says, "Thank you!" I said, "What?" He replies, "Thank you so much! I survived this year in this bad economy due to the things you taught me. I'd never had made it without the tools you gave me. There's no one there now that can teach me what you taught me. I am very grateful." To hear his words makes me feel so good. That is the part of the job I loved the most; to help and inspire others.

Just a few months ago I stopped in the old center. I saw one of the first salesmen I hired. He sat at his desk, looked up at me and said, "Look at this, Terri." He holds up a positive saying I had distributed years earlier in a meeting about attitude. He tells me how often he looks at this quote as a reminder and how much he appreciates me. I feel grateful for the impact I had on so many people.

By now, I've listened to so many authors that have opened me up to the many possibilities this life offers. Gregg Braden is a scientist and a spiritualist. His books amaze me. There are too many to mention them all here. His book Unleashing the Power of the God Code tells of the ancient message, and the name of God, that is encoded in the cells of our body. He explains the lost key that allows DNA to be translated into language. Also, how to switch the healing codes of your body to 'ON.' In another one of his books The Divine

Matrix he tells how our feelings are the language of our Universe. This makes me wonder about the years I had lived detached from my feelings. How did that hurt me and my life? Also, all the years I spent in 'limp mode.' His books are brilliant in many ways and have expanded my mind.

I've listened to so many of Gregg Braden and Dr. Dyer's books I feel I know these men personally. Another insightful book is by Bruce H. Lipton Ph.D. entitled The Biology of Belief. This book tells the science of just why our beliefs create our world, and this information fascinates me. All the more reason I need to change my beliefs.

Think and Grow Rich by Napoleon Hill is another great masterpiece. I hear it over and over again how our thoughts shape our world. Many things these books tell me to do I have done most of my life. This makes me feel good. Do all you can with what you have is one message I hear from many authors.

Wallace D Wattles in The Science of Getting Rich defines the science of wealth attraction. The foundation idea is "There's a thinking stuff from which all things are made… A thought in this substance, produces the thing that is imagined by the thought." All this information settles in my mind.

During this period of time I begin to feel I'm not making as much progress with the meditation as I'd like. I do feel many benefits as far as peace and concentration. But, I don't see my beliefs changing in any way. I feel stagnant. I ask God, "What's going on with me?" I soon have a dream. This dream is the most incredible dream of my life to date. The dream feels very real to me. I even ask myself in my dream, am I awake? I assure myself I am asleep. In the dream I am lying in the most lush, green grass I've ever seen. An eye appears in the sky, just one large eye. I watch the eye as the color of the iris keeps changing. Then I rise up to the eye and am staring into it directly. I have a really good feeling. Then I wake up.

The meaning of the green grass is good fortune and happiness according to my dream books. All nature dreams of trees, flowers, etc. are good omens, as long as they're in bloom and healthy. The meaning is the opposite if they are dying. An eye looking at you, according to my dream book, is a secret admirer, God. Reading this explanation gives me a chill all over. I now know my progress is just fine.

Soon after that dream my house is hit by lightning. The next day when the electrician looks over everything, I notice the items that are damaged, and all seems very strange to me. All the GFI outlets in the house are burnt. My refrigerator motor is hit. Also, the area in my master bath that affects my vanity and blow dryer are dead. I get the thought; this looks like it's the thyroid of my home. My mind lights up with the thought that my thyroid is healing! I know many think I'm crazy, but this is my view.

I go to work and announce my thyroid is healing. My house is struck by lightning. I'm getting rewired, a new motor in my refrigerator, and I see this miracle happen right before my eyes. I'm healing. Everyone at work knows not to argue with me in this state. They just say "Ok Terri, whatever you say." I am convinced I see the signs of healing power, and I give thanks to God. My son tells me not to mention this to anyone. They'll think you're crazy. I told him, "Too late for that!" I learned a great line from Dr. Dyer, "Whatever anyone thinks of me is none of my business." I love this quote and remember it often. Besides, no one can prove me wrong. Everything is relative. Everything is energy. These are my thoughts and this is how I think. Besides, these are fun, happy thoughts. Use your imagination for something fun.

To help myself heal, I also go to church to have the anointing for the sick. I just know I'm getting better. No doubt. And sure enough by the time the six months is over, my thyroid is back to the normal range. Yes! I'm so happy I listened to myself when so many told me this feat could not be done. I do the happy dance for days. Many do not believe me. Perhaps the first blood test was wrong I am told, but

I know for a fact how I feel, and I know I am healed. I do not need anyone else's validation. I know.

Towards the end of the year in one of my meditations I see the building I work in with another name on it. This is the first vision I've ever had during meditation. I'm a bit stunned. When I arrive at work, I only tell one person what I saw. "I'm not sure how, but I know an ownership change is imminent," I tell him. The store will be sold. I'm actually thinking the center may be sold to my brother-in-law. He and I have had several conversations with the owner over the past few years about buying the store. The owner said when he's ready, he'll let us know. I think possibly this is why I had the vision.

In January, the owner makes the announcement that he sold the store to a local company that has other franchises. Everyone where I work goes into panic mode. The owner tells the group of employees not to ask any questions because he doesn't know the answers. The atmosphere in the center quickly changes into a stress mess. The fear of the unknown causes many to think the worst. I assure everyone they are safe. Usually only the managers get the boot. I still think the sale may be going to my brother-in-law. I've seen many deals go down before papers are signed. I still have hope. I had a vision for a reason.

The months ahead get stressful. No one can concentrate on the job at hand. Rumors of what is coming start to circulate. Many employees know people from the new owner's store. The Mercedes store is only a block away. I hear the name of my replacement through the grapevine in February. I confront the owner, and he is shocked I know this man's name, but he assures me I will have a job. My future employment situation is out of my hands. There's nothing I can do but the job at hand. I do my best to calm my co-workers. I know I will be all right. I know God has my back, always. One foot in front of the other, here I go again.

Please, follow along. My life-long miracle will reveal itself soon.

Be Curious

Be curious about who you are
Keep searching and dig deep, down far
Everyone is a shining star
Let go, and energize all that you are

Shine your light and let it glow
The radiance grows; this is your show
Let go of all grief, let go of all strife
With every new day, create a happy life

Energy flows where attention goes
Now's your chance to reap what you sow
Intend what you want; watch all you do
All will be well when you intend it to

Do all you can, and watch what you say
Pay attention to what you're creating today
Be curious, and focus on positive things
Thoughts become things, let a new life begin

Cruise 2006 top left: Dan, Jerome. bottom left: Terri, Theresa

"Nothing comes from without. All comes from within."

- Neville Goddard

Chapter X

Letting Go

Let it all go
Rise and Shine
Here in this moment
All is fine
Don't burden carrying
All of time

Let it all go
And be smart
Each and every sunrise
Grants you a new start
Energize today
Live with all your heart

April 11, 2010 is the first meeting with the new owners. I clearly see they have no position of value to present to me. Without an interview, not even a question, they offer me a straight sales position in another one of their stores - no demo, no gas, knowing it would not be acceptable. It is not uncommon.

After the meeting is over, I proceed downstairs to my office and start packing my things. There's no reason to stay. The changeover is not scheduled to happen until the first of May, but with no future and no severance pay, it is not worth my time to stay. The atmosphere is toxic to say the least. All the employees are worried about their jobs, their pay, and what the change of ownership will bring for them. Fear of the unknown grips them. As positive as I usually am, I didn't care to handle their stresses on top of my own uncertainty.

I make my rounds and say good-bye to my wonderful co-workers. It is a sad time, and many people are shocked. I give them reassurance as best I can that their future is secure. Only the sales manager's position is affected. They will be fine. With that I make my exit.

Driving home, I feel so free. Never before had I felt so locked into a job, even though I had liked my work. Two days later my unemployed thirty-four year old son Dan and I pack the car and head to Florida where two of my sisters have winter homes very close to each other. The trip takes two days, and we have fun along the way. This trip is a test run for our planned excursion next month to California where we intend to check out employment possibilities, visit friends, and see the sights.

Our drive to Florida is easy, and we are with our family in no time. I haven't taken a road trip in years, and we have a great time relaxing with family. We bike, boat, swim, dine and shop as well as visit the beach. I have not been on a bike in quite a few years, and even though I fall a few times, I love it.

On one shopping excursion my son drives my sisters Rosemary and Anne and me to Naples. As we walk along 5th Avenue, we decide to enter a women's clothing store. Dan says, "I will wait for you here." The store has an open-air front along the sidewalk. I stop at the first rack with my back to the street. All of a sudden I hear a huge SNAP, a noise so loud and close I jump in panic.

I quickly turn and see that a palm tree has snapped in half across the sidewalk; an SUV had run off the road and plowed down the tree. People gather around to see if anyone is injured. My heart sinks because the tree landed in the exact spot where my son had been standing just seconds earlier. I do not immediately see my son, and my heart stops.

I rush outside and search for Dan. Finally, I see him walking towards me, and tears start to stream down my face and my body shakes with relief. Those past several seconds had felt like an hour to my heart. My sister Anne, on the other side of the clothes rack, had been facing the street and knew that Danny was not in any danger, but she could not relay that to me as everything happened so fast. I was so very happy and grateful in that moment that I stopped in a shop to buy a heart charm for my bracelet to remember my happy heart. My sisters and I had been standing in the exact spot the SUV hit less than a minute prior to the accident. We all count our blessings. Luckily, no one is hurt in the accident. The driver of the car had lost consciousness, and that is why the SUV plowed onto the sidewalk and mowed down the tree.

Later that afternoon I relax by the pool at my sister Rosemary's house. I tell my brother-in-law Jack about the accident and how grateful I am that we are all safe. I also mention how grateful I am for the free time I now have and how I feel so unencumbered.

Jack says, "It's easy to be grateful for something you receive or are blessed with, but try being grateful for something you wanted but did not get. That is not as easy." That thought intrigues me, and I file it away for another time.

When I tell my sister Rosemary about our plans to drive out West, she shares her experience of the long and sometimes tedious drive, and so we decide it might be a better plan to fly and rent a car, and that is what we do.

After returning home from Florida and celebrating Mother's Day (I am not going to miss that day with my family), Dan and I fly to

Las Vegas, and the fun begins immediately. Fun in the sun, dinner, shows, we did it all. After three days in Vegas, we rent an SUV and drive to the Grand Canyon, proceed to Lake Havisu, then to Long Beach, California. We both have friends in Long Beach, and we stay there for four days. This is our halfway point. Danny says, "Even if the rest of the trip sucks, it is still the best trip ever!" We really are enjoying this time together.

The rest of the trip is awesome as well. We take a few days to drive up the coast visiting Malibu and Monterey enjoying the scenery. We end our trip with five days in San Francisco. This travel experience has been a great adventure, and I count my blessings the whole way. I never before had this sort of time to spend traveling and just love it.

We return home at the end of May. It's now time to find the right job. I have no doubt that I will find a job quickly, even with a horrible economy. I begin sending out resumes and making calls. I know for sure that God has my back. I only need to do my part. I know and believe with all my heart that whatever my future holds, it will be great.

In between the job hunting I ponder some ideas that I have trouble understanding. Many of the books I have read and listened to over the past four years mention that all things already exist in our Universe. So the book I intend to write already exists somewhere in the Universe? How is that so? This information is difficult for me to understand; yet I believe it's true because it comes from reliable sources. The concept is hard for me to grasp, so I ask God to help me comprehend.

It still amazes me; every time God finds a way to answer me. Several weeks later I sit down to watch TV. I check my DVR recordings. One of the shows I like is "The Big Bang Theory." I click on that title. However, the DVR had recorded a different show titled "The

Big Bang" from the Discovery Channel. Watching the show I see just how the Universe started with a big bang. Seeing the huge container, our Universe, explode with energy I understand how our Universe holds all things. All matter is present in the initial bang. Matter just keeps changing form and expanding. I comprehend how we are all One. From nothing, energy comes into form. There's the answer to my prayer, clear as day. Now I comprehend just how all matter, anything that is now here or will be here in the future, already exists.

Seems interesting how the most important information I receive, ideas that change or enlighten me in some way, come to me as a gift or as an event that I stumble upon. I now understand that if I have the desire to do or create something, it's already contained in the Universe. I get it. All I need is the energy of my thoughts, words, and actions to form the matter and attract it to me. Our whole Universe consists of matter that's constantly changing.

Getting back to the business of the job search and being open to moving for the right job, I get my house ready to put on the market, just in case. It's obvious there are not many jobs in my area, and I am open for the right job wherever it is, feeling certain that whatever is next for me will be spectacular. I feel it. I even tell a friend that whatever is ahead for me is going to put to use my whole life experience. This I know for sure.

Every day I send out resumes and write cover letters. I network as never before. My credentials are excellent. However, I am not getting many responses. But I still do all I can every day. That is my part. With each cover letter I write my strength and confidence expand. I promise myself I will not settle. The door will open when it is my job. I have faith, and I will not worry. Worry, you know, is a misuse of your imagination.

Many friends remark about how at ease I am during this time of crisis. Most people in my position show signs of stress. However, my faith, along with my personal history, keeps me grounded. I will survive. I am on a guided path, and I know it. Whatever happens is meant to be. In addition, I am enjoying every minute. Every day I wake up in joy and say out loud, "Thank You for another day of freedom!" This is truly how I feel. Free! I am able to exercise on my treadmill, meditate, go to the gym, take long leisurely walks, and enjoy time with family and friends. At the same time I push and push to keep my focus on the job hunt. I know all I have to do is my part, and God will do the rest. I have no doubt. God's got my back, pushing me forward with determination. I believe something great is coming my way.

Over the summer months I often visit my friends' pool to enjoy their 'little piece of heaven.' Carole and Andre` are a few of my dance friends. I'm grateful they share some time with me. On several occasions Carole has asked me, "What would you do if you could do anything?" My answer is always the same, "Be a writer." However, I always thought that I needed a job for security, a very limiting thought but at this point I have allowed it to hold me back-but not for long. My words start flowing out of my mouth as I speak with passion about my ideas.

Towards the end of June I have another vision during meditation. I see my cell phone with my angel-friend's name in the caller ID. I laugh out loud. I think it must be wishful thinking. He's been gone for three years, and we lost touch after the first year. I haven't heard from him in two years.

To my surprise, I get a call from him soon after my vision. He's returning to the area for a wedding and is checking to see if I'd like to see him. Of course, it's always a pleasure to catch up with an old friend. His visit lasts for seven weeks, and we spend plenty of time together. It's as if he had never left. Looking back, I am so grateful I entered that relationship. Hesitation and fear almost blocked it, but now I have cherished memories to last a lifetime.

Somehow, even with my faith and trust, by the middle of July I feel some anxiety. It's very unusual for me, and a feeling with which I'm not comfortable. I put calls out to several people about different jobs. No one responds. Also, I've been overlooked for a job I was more than qualified for. My anxiety level increases with each passing day.

My sister Anne and her husband Craig are back from Florida and staying at their summer home on the Delaware Bay. I call Anne to see if I can visit. My plan is to get away for a few days to take my mind off the job search. With her affirmative answer I am packed and on the road in a few hours. Their new home is on the waterfront, and I so appreciate their hospitality and spending time with them.

At home once again the anxiety returns and remains all week regardless of what I do to shake it. I exercise, meditate, pray, but I cannot shake this bad feeling. This unsettled feeling upsets me because I believe it shows a lack of trust in God. By the end of the week, I decide to go to confession because to me it's disrespectful to God to have anxiety. First, I know that when I am anxious, Divine Guidance cannot get through easily. Secondly, I know that if I trust God, there is no need for anxiety. I do trust God, so what is going on? After confession, I feel somewhat better. However, the next day I realize that the anxiety started and most likely was caused by a new meditation level.

There are different levels of the meditation program I do. I began a new level a few weeks prior to my anxiety attack, and sometimes an anxious phase can result. Chaos can surface, sometimes emotionally, sometimes physically. The chaos keeps building until the nervous system adjusts and makes a shift. After my system shifts, I feel much better. Now, I understand what happened, and I know my anxiety was not an insult to God. I feel much better in every way. About the same time, in one of my meditations, I have a vision of 'a skeleton key.' I have no idea what this key symbol represents, but I am certain that it is significant because I rarely see images. I tuck this image away and wait to see what develops.

In August, I hear through the grapevine of a job that will soon be available very close to home. This position is a shoe-in for me. I know some of the people at the dealership from my years in the business. I believe this is the job for me -another BMW center about a half hour's drive- no move required. For sure this is the one God is saving for me. I know the president of this company very well. However, he has the reputation of never returning calls, and I know that reaching him will be a challenge, especially because this job is not yet advertised.

After many calls and several emails, I receive an email from this gentleman stating that he's not sure how he will fill the position. He may promote someone from within the company. He will keep me posted. So, I send him an email every week to keep in touch, highlighting my strengths to let him know why he should hire me. He eventually invites me in to speak with him, more of a courtesy because he knows me. He will let me know what he decides to do. In the meantime, I do all I can do to keep in touch with him in a professional manner.

In late August I receive The Power by Rhonda Byrne as a birthday gift. This book discusses the law of attraction. As I turn one of the pages in the book I see the 'key' from my meditation a few weeks earlier. It literally jumps off the page at me, and I take notice. The key is depicted in a section of the book that speaks of gratitude. I read this chapter a few times knowing there is important information here. "It's no wonder I don't have a job yet," I thought after reading this book. I get up every day and give thanks for my new found freedom. With true joy and gratitude, I give thanks for my freedom. The book tells me that gratitude is the great multiplier. Everyday my gratitude just expands my freedom. I have to laugh at this fact. It also reminds me of the conversation I had with my brother-in-law Jack in

Florida. Be grateful for what you did not get. I start thinking. My wheels are really turning. What is the meaning I am meant to see? I know when I ask the question, the answer will come.

I look back at my life and think of the sadness that I endured. I remember how I still tried to find the positive and how I found something for which I was grateful every day. I can see clearly how gratitude changed my life dramatically. By showing appreciation, my entire life just got better and better. Gratitude is the main ingredient for making my life as fantastic as it is today. Coupled with a positive focus, and doing all I can, the good in my life keeps expanding. When I review the book again, I notice that the key appears on a few other pages before the section on gratitude. Funny how it went unnoticed until I got to the chapter on gratitude. It's no mistake. I received the right message.

Now I start to think about all the jobs that passed me by. I focus on being grateful for not getting those jobs. Some are easy to feel grateful for because I didn't want them. A couple others I need more time before the gratitude can surface. I'm going to work on becoming genuinely grateful I tell myself as I tuck that thought away.

As thoughts of gratitude graze over my life history, my vision becomes clear. I have always kept reminders in front of me to give gratitude for all the past events of my life. If you come to my home and walk up to the second level, you will see my best reminders of gratitude. I have the memories of family, friends, and many great experiences in my life on display. Every time I walk up the stairs I see a multitude of photos. I have photos on the wall, a table full of pictures, a bench full of memories, and even more on the floor. I can't walk by without feeling blessed and grateful for my wonderful life. There's also an artist's picture of the Christ Child from my parents' home. The picture had hung over their mantle in their living room. Now it serves as the center of my photo wall. I always give thanks as I look at this picture. It is a reminder to me that Christ is the center of my life, and that thought always makes me feel good.

I also keep fresh flowers on my table. Every time I walk downstairs I see the flowers and feel the joy they give me. The only time I may not have flowers is if they are not fresh when I go to buy them. Flowers are one of my favorite things in life. At one point in my life I found myself feeling a bit down because I had no one to buy me flowers. It didn't take me long to see what a ridiculous thought that was. I can buy my own flowers. And that is what I do.

Until I read The Power and saw 'the key' from my meditation, it never really struck me before just how gratitude has influenced and enhanced my life. It just comes naturally to me. Even during the sad years I was grateful for what I had and for the help I received from above in getting through the days. After the sadness, my gratitude just multiplied for the life I had gained. My gratitude has always been real and heartfelt.

With the realization that gratitude is the great multiplier, I ask myself if I should stop being grateful about my present freedom in order to find a job? Can I possibly not be grateful for this free time? No, because it would not be genuine. My gratitude keeps exploding for this life of freedom I now have, and not being locked into a job with those long hours. I love the life I am living. Is it possible to find a job with this attitude, I wonder.

With all these thoughts swirling through my mind, there's more happening within. It's now the last week in August and I have three dreams that warn me that something bad is coming. Never having had warning dreams before, I pay close attention. My father is in one dream, my sister Kathleen is in another, and the third contains a severe warning. All three dreams, when interpreted by my dream books, give a warning to be on the lookout for a horrific act, treacherous even. I haven't a clue. What can it possibly mean? I get very concerned and pray for guidance to figure it out.

In early September my friend Pat and I go to Atlantic City to enjoy the spa at the Borgata and spend a few days at the beach. The weather is just glorious at the Jersey shore. The first day we head to the spa for massages. We pamper ourselves, one of my favorite things to do. Then we relax in the hot tubs all afternoon. In the evening we go out for some cocktails and a relaxing dinner. When I fall asleep that night, I have the most horrific dream ever.

Upon waking, I finally understand the treacherous act I'd been warned about in my earlier dreams. I am shaken, and at the same time very grateful that Pat is there to talk to, a real Godsend. She is very insightful, and I tell her about my dream. I am standing in a kitchen with a young girl to my right. I do not recognize the little girl. I'd say she is about six or seven. She stands and watches me cut off my left thumb. The scene is very matter of fact with no emotion. I put the knife in my left hand and tell her I am going to need her help. As I put the knife to my right wrist, I start to cut off my right hand. I look at her and say, "I need help with the knife because my left hand is weak without the thumb." Together we make the cut, and we slice off my right hand. With that, I put gauze around the stump, put it through the straps of my purse, open the door and say "Come on honey, let's go." No emotion at all, just matter of fact.

This dream horrifies me. What can the dream mean? I know it's something significant due to the dreams warning me to look out for it. I am very upset to say the least. At the same time I am very grateful that this horrible act came to me as a dream and not as an actual event. Pat thinks the dream may allude to the dejection I feel by not being hired for so many jobs. Even people I know have let me down. She thinks I may feel that people cut me off, hence the amputation. I think perhaps she may be on the right track, but in my mind the job situation isn't horrifying. Disappointing yes, but not treacherous. I have no other explanation and am not sure what to make of it. I send up a little prayer for some insight.

Pat and I continue with our day, and the beach is just delightful, one of the best weather days I can ever remember at the Jersey shore. After a few hours in the sun I go for a swim in the ocean. Then the revelation hits me. As soon as I get wet, the answer flashes through my mind. This dream is about my past. When I made the decision to give up custody of my two young sons during the divorce, I thought that decision equaled cutting off my thumb. However, the reality turned out to be much worse. The consequence to that decision turned out to be as horrifying as losing my right hand and my left thumb. There was nothing I could do to change it at the time. I went on with my life emotionally detached. The little girl in my dream was about the same age as my youngest son at that time. Many times dreams reverse sexes according to my dream books, and I interpret the little girl in my dream to represent my son. I finally understand it. My mind now floods with memories of this past horror.

After my swim, I share my new insight with Pat. I am still shaking from the dream but feeling relieved that I at last understand the message. I have always felt guilty about needing so much help at that time in my life and ending up in a home for women when I had such a great start in life. My father told me that I broke his heart when I went away for help, and I always felt ashamed for my behavior back then and for causing my family pain.

The insight I prayed for enlightens me to the point that I realize that I had made the right decision during my divorce and had handled the consequences as best I could at the time. The warning dream where my dad appeared and warned me of this treachery, also gave a clue to coming happiness. According to my dream book if your father speaks to you in a dream, it is a sign of coming happiness. For the first time in my life, I had a positive feeling about decisions I had made in the past. This dream also opened a door that had been locked and sealed shut years ago. It felt eerie to have it open, but it cleared me in some way. It's hard for me to describe. Over the years I rarely spoke about the dark days of my life to anyone. I have always felt ashamed for being in need of such help. This dream gave me a new perspective.

When I return home, I fully open up to my past pain. I begin writing about the sad time of my life. I've never been able to go to that dark place before. I had only scratched the surface of the pain prior to that dream. It's still amazing to me that the dream broke through the barrier that had been off limits to my emotions. For the first time I write about my past pain with some depth. I write for several days until I feel somewhat released. Then it is right back to my diligent job hunt. I still needed a job…so I thought.

By mid-September I get an email that lets me know I did not get the job I was so sure had my name on it. I am stunned. It just had to be the job for me. It fit so well into my plan. What is God thinking? My mind is spinning with questions. I am very disappointed; yet I believe that God must have another plan that is not ready for me to see yet. I have no doubt. It's all meant to be. However, in the moment I feel dejected. I wonder what can possibly lie ahead for me. Where will I find the right job? When will the job show up? Time keeps moving on.

Now it's October. My job focus is ferociously strong. I network and am able to get an interview with a company out West. On October 13th I have a phone interview with this company at 5:30 pm, plus another interview in person, with another company the following day about three hours away. Waking up on the day of the phone interview I feel a little anxious. Not bad, but enough that I need to stop the feeling before it gets worse. I refuse to go down that anxiety-ridden road again.

During my morning prayers I usually pray to different saints and angels for specific people on my prayer list. On that particular day I pray to God and my usual angels and saints, only this time I pray just one prayer, "Thank you for helping me to let go and let God." My prayer is only to be able to let go. As I move forward with my usual day, I exercise and then check for any job news on the computer. I instantly notice an email from someone whom I've never received an email before. It's Hale Dwoskin, and he is selling a DVD entitled, "Letting Go." I get goose bumps immediately and have to walk away from the computer.

The email, and answer to my prayer, shakes me to the core. First crying and then laughing about how instantly and tangible my prayer has been answered, I hastily grab my wallet to purchase this DVD that mystically showed up in my email on this particular day. Normally, when purchasing a DVD on-line it takes up to a week for it to arrive in the mail. On this day, once I pay, I am able to watch it immediately by downloading it to my computer. After watching the instructional DVD I am able to let go and release my anxiety. It is a true miracle to me. The miracle that takes place this day is only part of the miracle from my prayer to 'let go and let God.' The other part of this miracle takes a few more weeks to manifest in my life.

The phone interview goes well, but in truth, I don't want to move out West. The next day I drive three hours for the other interview. This position is for General Manager in a Lexus center and will also require a move but would be close enough to see my family regularly. Upon my arrival someone takes my photo and proceeds to enlarge it to an 8 x 10 full face shot and staples the photo on top of my resume. It looks ridiculous. There's also a production line of candidates. Questioning the young woman why she enlarged the photo she told me so that her boss can easily recall the many candidates he is interviewing.

After waiting for over an hour, my turn arrives to speak with the man in charge. He asks me questions about how to run a sales desk. I tell him I am there to interview for the General Manager position.

He tells me point blank that I don't qualify. I remind him that according to the ad, I am qualified for the position. He tells me that he's also hiring a sales manager and a desk manager, but only ran one ad for the GM because he gets better candidates that way. It is the shortest interview ever. He tells me he is interviewing 200 people.

Now I am visibly upset. I had given up a beautiful day of freedom for nothing. A sales manager position isn't worth moving away from my family. What a waste of time. I am outraged over the false advertising. The ad had indicated that candidates with General Sales Manager's experience were welcome to apply. Driving home I decide that I need a vacation from job hunting. I start thinking about gratitude. Is it possible for me to become grateful for all the jobs I did not get? I am grateful that this job did not pan out because I really don't' want to move; that is now clear to me. I make a decision in that moment not to move. I already spend enough time away from my family.

My thoughts then turn to the conversation I had with my brother-in-law Jack about gratitude many months ago. I look back over my life and remember things I had wanted that I did not get. Being grateful for what I didn't get puts a different spin on my thoughts. My thinking starts to change. Could I possibly be grateful for what happened with my children and the sadness that I lived through for years? That is going to take some time and thought. I am not sure I am capable of being grateful for that terrible time, but decide to keep an open mind.

My vacation from job hunting is liberating, and after a week of not thinking about a job I decide I need another week off. I just enjoy my life along with the beautiful fall weather in Pennsylvania. Relaxed in total joy I realize I am living the life I've always wanted. This is the life of my dreams doing all the things I heard Dr. Dyer talk about in one of his audio books. Every time he got to the part where he speaks of his lifestyle, how he walks up to three hours a day, swims, does yoga and just enjoys life, I always say "Yes!" That is what I'd love to do! Here I am doing all these things and loving every minute of it. The only difference is that Dr. Dyer also mentions he has so much money coming in he doesn't know what to do with it. This I do not have…YET! However, it does get me thinking. For now, I have what I need.

I now recall what God says in Communion with God by Neale Donald Walsch. God says, "There is no need." It is the first of the ten illusions God reveals in this book. I now see, in this moment, I have all I need. In reality, I have more than I need. In the same book God also says to meditate and exercise. This I also do and am feeling very good about myself.

For over a week since I asked for help in 'letting go and letting God,' I feel a blockage in my abdominal area. It feels like an energy ball in my gut. I try to stretch and meditate to loosen the feeling but nothing I do seems to help. It becomes more intense with each passing day. Finally, after a week I ask God, "OK, what is this wrenching feeling about?" The answer shocks me. It's the pain of my past resurfacing. All these years I've told myself that the pain I suffered from missing my children is NEVER going away. The saying 'time heals all wounds' doesn't apply to my sadness. Nothing can ever heal this pain because the time with my young children is gone forever. It is NEVER coming back. The pain is here to stay. That is what I always believed.

For twenty-five years that limiting belief has been holding me back and blocking my own power. I had thought it was just a fact of life. I didn't dwell on it. I buried those feelings deep inside. I closed and locked the door, and tossed away the key. I believed all those years that's just the way it was. I rarely spoke of the pain I endured. Had I given them the chance, the emotions would have erupted. Instead I held onto the fear, deep inside, knowing that if I opened that door, this volcano of emotion might erupt, so I kept it tightly locked.

Now I finally see the truth. Becoming aware of this limiting belief is what allows me to let go. By following the 'letting go' process described in Hale Dwoskin's DVD, I let the pain go. No volcano erupted and I didn't need years of therapy. What's more amazing is how wonderful I felt afterward. Immediately, my spirit lifted. All my feelings became more amplified. All of a sudden the block of energy in my gut dissipated and was gone. It's hard to believe that it just dissolved the way it did. To me, this release is the second miracle that stems from my prayer to let go and let God.

Tears of happiness run down my cheeks. I feel so free and now have much more room for good feelings inside me. This experience amazes me still. I see clearly that for the past twenty-five years I have been living in 'limp' mode, only feeling partially the emotions life offers. Holding all the pain down within took so much energy. How did I accomplish all I did with this blockage? It stuns me to think of it. All this time the pain was under the surface. I've been happy and grateful for my life here in the present moment. I have been truly happy. I didn't dwell on the pain or feel like a victim. I just lived with the pain having no idea how much space it required inside me. This blockage slowed progress in all my meditation work, but now it is gone.

I decide that another week off from the job search is warranted when an event occurs that forces me to slow down. About four in the morning I get out of bed to use the bathroom. As I stand, a dizzy spell causes me to sit on the bed for a bit. Rising, I cautiously begin walking with my left hand on the bed for support. After taking about five small steps, I stop to regain balance. I began walking very slowly with caution, and BAM, all of a sudden I'm on the floor. My feet fly right out from under me with force. My head hit the arm of a chair. Some energy source I can't see sweeps my feet out from under me. I hit hard. I suffer a whiplash, and the jolt badly bruises my shoulder. I go to my chiropractor three times a week for months. The injury stops me from dancing and swimming. I do some walking but not nearly as much.

Many new thoughts and beliefs begin to flow to me. The gate inside me opens. Thoughts from my meditation work start flashing in my mind. New beliefs appear; limiting beliefs disappear. My mind kicks into overdrive, and my feelings intensify. My channels become clear, and new ideas emerge. I begin to believe that all things are possible. I see my future path clearly; I suddenly have a bird's eye view of my entire life, and can visualize the total future picture.

After referring to a few meditation books, I make a new discovery. My relentless job search along with my fierce workout routine actually blocked me from my own progress. Such strong focus creates resistance. Only when I took a break from my job search were the changes able to surface. Hence the phrase "Don't hold the flower too tight." All the changes taking place are the result of being forced to slow down because of my accidental fall and learning to let go. I'm now ready to receive the third part of the 'letting go' miracle.

Without my limiting beliefs I see clearly that it is time to start a new venture and end my job search. I recall the God-sent message several years ago that I would someday write about my life. I am a writer. This is what I'm meant to do. I have notebooks full of material. Although I have no idea how to make it happen, I have the ***belief*** that I can do it. I make the announcement to my family and friends, I am a writer. I have my new career path. Many think I am off my rocker, but most are supportive.

The gratitude I feel swells in me. Incredibly I'm able to look at my past sadness and begin to be grateful for it. I believe now that my earlier difficulties served a good purpose. Once I get to the point of being grateful for my entire life, my thoughts and feelings change. I immediately have a better understanding of what 'the key' from my meditation fully means, and my entire world begins to shift.

My whole life makes more sense. I now understand pain and what acceptance of pain accomplishes. Once I accept the pain, there is no more suffering. I understand that deciding to be happy during my sadness had changed my life, and my gratitude multiplied all in my life. Acceptance is what allows for growth. Since I finally understand the meaning of my life, I am capable of helping others.

This period is a physically painful period. My emotions ride a roller coaster. Every feeling, good and bad, is intensified. In addition, several of my loved ones are experiencing major problems in their lives, and I empathize with them. As I begin writing, it feels as if every muscle in my back is pulling at me telling me to stop. At first I do not realize what is happening to me, but then it soon becomes clear. My body has spent twenty-five years holding the pain down and out of sight, and now all of a sudden, I am writing about that pain. My body is trying to stop me.

After a few months with my chiropractor, Dr. Brian Capaldi, there hasn't been much improvement. He is very concerned and suggests muscle therapy. Here enters another angel in my life, Jeff Myers of Universal Massage Arts. Jeff possesses a magical way with energy and touch. He intuitively knows what to do. He helps me in the moment when I am there, but the fix doesn't hold. After a month with him there's still no progress. Brian suggests that I go for tests. He knows me well enough to know that there must be a reason why my body doesn't respond. I am healthy, and my body should be bouncing back. I tell him of my energy release and my physical reaction to writing; he now thinks we should give the treatments a little more time. Once I realize what's going on in my body, my healing begins and I make progress. It is slow, painful progress. Pain still surfaces when I write. My muscles freak out about letting this energy out after they worked so hard for years to keep it in.

I return for more muscle therapy, and my body begins to mend, not completely but getting better. The sessions are intense. The therapist digs deep into the tissue. I'm left with more bruises. There is one session where he goes deep into one spot and holds it a long time. My emotions release and tears start flowing uncontrollably. As the tears roll down my cheeks, memories of my past pain flash through my mind, and I feel the release. As my pain begins to release I have more memories rise of another trauma long forgotten, lashes of being beaten by the man I loved and lived with. These memories were buried in the locked vault within me and barely noticed due to the horror of losing my children. The pain of losing my children trumped all else. This is why I call Jeff an angel in my life. He's clearing my energy. He is very gifted, and I am so grateful for his help. I believe that the reason I am working my way deep into my emotions is so that I will be able to write of my past horror. My energy is slowly clearing, and I begin letting go of all resistance, finally.

When I arrive home, I ice some of the tender spots Jeff worked on. I am in shock. The memories of my past beatings are devastating to recall. I dealt with this situation earlier with my counselors at the home for women, but the impact of the seriousness of the situation was overshadowed, due to the pain I felt from my sons moving away. I have such an incredible feeling inside with the release of all this negative energy. I am amazed at how wonderfully free I feel, outside of the sore spots under the ice pack.

Comprehending just how painful my past is, I now understand exactly how I managed my way through the pain. I see what a wonderful life I have had for many years. Had I not put a focus on something positive, been grateful for what I had whether I liked my life or not, and disciplined myself to do all I could every day, there would be no happy memories staring at me every time I walk up the stairwell in my home. I might still be wallowing in the sadness, suffering, and waiting for a miracle to change my life.

Many miracles have changed my life when I wasn't looking. I took action and decided to be happy right where I was even though the sadness was a horrible and devastating time for me. I decided to be happy in the moment, no matter what. Choosing to be happy had created a better future for me. Looking back I am so grateful for the foundation of faith and love into which I was born. As I have said many times, my family is my biggest blessing. Without faith and love I would not have made it through the sadness as well as I did.

Becoming grateful for my past pain also enlightened me to the benefit of exactly what I learned living in that home for women. I received intense therapy 24/7; the days were long, and the residents were not friends to each other. However, now I see that I gained an understanding of others' pain. We participated in group sessions daily, sometimes twice a day. We were in a group together from seven in the morning until ten at night. An hour of privacy had to be earned. Only now can I appreciate what I gained from that experience.

God is brilliant! Blindly I walked into hell due to a consequence of a decision that He clearly guided. All these years I've felt that I'd gone astray back then, and only in becoming grateful for the hell am I able to see that I did the best I could at the time. One of my meditation books entitled <u>Twenty-Four Hours a Day</u> states: *The laws of nature are unchangeable. Often people get angry with God for allowing a good person to get sick or for natural disasters, but God does not interfere with the working of natural laws. As far as natural laws are concerned, God makes no distinction between good people and bad people. Sickness and death may strike anywhere. The spiritual laws are also made for us to obey. Our choice of good or evil decides whether we go upward to true success in life or downward to loss and defeat.* Many people put God out of their life for an experience they perceive as bad. My prayer during my divorce was for the best choice for my sons, and that choice brought consequences for me. Only now am I free in understanding, I did the best I could in dealing with those consequences. For the first time, I feel good about my past. Grateful for the choice I made.

There's a Scripture reading I've heard for many years in church. I never truly comprehended the full meaning. I heard it again several months ago. The reading presents two women who are washing dishes and one woman is taken away. Then the reading describes a similar scenario for two men working in a field, and one is taken away. This time I ask God what the scripture means. I receive the answer that when we make a decision, we can choose with our higher self or our lower self; both live within us. With each choice we make, one is taken away and the other remains. We are continuously choosing our path and can go either way with every decision we make. I'm so grateful for my life's mantra: "Thank You for helping me to make the choices that bring me closer to You."

I have a lifetime full of wonderful experiences and memories because of the choice I made every day to be happy, no matter what. The sadness is still a part of my past, and always will be, but even with the sadness buried in me, I didn't dwell on it. I put focus on the positive, and I flourished. In Communion with God our Creator speaks to us through the author, Neale Donald Walsch. God tells us:

> *Happiness is a decision, not an experience. You can decide to be happy without what you thought you needed in order to be happy, and you will be. Your experience is the result of your decision, not the cause of it.*

Choosing happiness is exactly what I did years ago. I made a decision to be happy. My life wasn't at all what I wanted, and at the time I even hated the circumstances of my life. I was so sad on the inside. But choosing happiness in the moment and giving thanks daily created a life of joy for me in the end. I had to focus on the present moment and find something in front of me to be happy about.

Gratitude helped me feel better. I couldn't change reality. I could only change my focus or my thoughts about the situation. Being happy made me feel better and more able to cope. I can't imagine where I'd be today had I lived my life differently.

I am so grateful the door to a job didn't open. I'm right where I'm meant to be. My beliefs now open the door to all possibilities. I'm living the life of my dreams. I'm a writer and believe I can do anything I choose. The income will come, I know it. I believe the way will be shown to me, and I will do my part to make it happen. A friend of mine recently told me how lucky I was because God guides me. She felt left out of the blessings I talk about. But the Divine navigation system is not unique to me. Guidance is there for all of us. To receive direction, you must open the door to your own spirit. Acknowledge its presence in your life and honor your spirit.

I've set my goal in the Divine navigation system to become a writer. I am doing all I can everyday with what is in front of me. I search the web to get as much information as I can find. There are a few contests that offer writer's training. I sign up for them. That is the impetus behind this book. It makes no matter if I win or lose. The book is written, and you are reading it. Mission accomplished. I've never been happier in my life outside of becoming a mom. With every word I write, I see and believe more and more that I'm going to succeed. I don't know how. I just know if I keep doing all I can, the rest will happen. It doesn't matter how long it takes. I see from my past, once I set the goal and hold the belief my goal is possible, it all will come to pass. This or something better will come as long as I do all I can. This is the job in front of me now.

For years I've been saying, "When you feel good, good things happen." Only I hadn't a clue as to how much better I was capable of feeling. I have been happy for many years and didn't fully ***feel*** all that I was capable of feeling. Dr. Dyer says, "Feel good and you feel God." I can definitely feel God more fully now.

Hindsight shows just how gratitude was the key to all I accomplished. It's with gratitude and a positive attitude that I became able to climb out of my rut and move forward. With a positive focus I kept moving in the right direction. I see how my whole career just spiraled up. It's all due to the gratitude I gave for my life every day. Gratitude is what multiplied the good in my life.

Here is a real kicker. Twenty-five years ago when I was in the home for women, my therapist took me on an internal journey with a meditation session she narrated. The meditation took me inside myself to ask what I needed to know. The answer I got is just what set me free today, 'Let Go' was the message I received then. I thought I did let go at that time, but now I see that I was blocked from letting go completely. It took me another twenty-five years to become aware of the limiting belief that was holding me back. That is one reason I'm writing this book. Maybe you will find a miracle in your life sooner than I did. Have you gone deep within? Are you willing to look inside?

I have gone deep within, and I intend to keep on going deeper because of this next experience I will share with you. This experience has changed me forever. Very early in the New Year, January 2011, my son and his wife face a tragic episode which leaves me feeling helpless. Unable to sleep I sit at the computer writing for nearly ten hours. My body screams at me with pain and muscle tension to stop. Finally, I take a break and try to rest. My muscles ache and so does my heart for my family in crisis. There is nothing I can do but pray.

The snow outside my window is fresh from yesterday's storm, and the air is very cold. I soak in a hot tub of Epsom salts to sooth my muscles. After soaking, I wrap myself in warmth and sit on my bed. I close my eyes to meditate for about twenty-five minutes. When I open my eyes, I see the most beautiful sight of my entire life. In the mirror across from me I see the reflection of a luminescent figure leaning over me, looking down at me as if to comfort me. This image is pure light, pure spirit and total feminine energy. The image is purified beauty; Unaltered love. I am in awe. As I turn to look directly at this beautiful sight, the spirit retracts in a swift motion and disappears into my body, right into the area of my heart.

In the moment, a calm peace comes over me. I take a few days before I speak or write about this life-changing event. I need to process what happened. I come to the conclusion that I had seen my soul. I often say to God when I see the power of a tree or a beautiful flower, "Thank You for allowing me to see Your beauty in all things." Now, I've seen God's beauty within myself. This is the most incredible gift I could ever receive; A miracle to me, for sure. My heart somehow knows my family will be all right. There is a long road ahead before the crisis will end, but all will be well. I feel this now. Sometimes a little rain must fall before a rainbow appears, and the tears we shed today will provide a brilliant rainbow to shield us, once the sun shines again. This too shall pass.

The main feeling I am left with months after this extraordinary experience is peace. Peace on earth can be attained if everyone just took time to honor his or her own soul. As I mentioned earlier, plugging into the power of the Soul gives you the power of the universe, and if everyone plugged into his or her own power, peace on earth would become very possible in a very short time. As the quote at the beginning of this chapter states; all comes from within. Within each of us lies the power to change the world. Let's do it together.

God is love, and He created life for all of us to be happy and to feel good. In The Power Rhonda Byrne makes the point that in order to create and attract good into your life, you need to be at least fifty-one percent in the positive, which is to feel good. We are all meant to feel joy. Gratitude is the key to generating good feelings. When we are full of the positive feelings of gratitude and love, all the negatives fade away. There's no room for anything negative when you are full of love. The Power also claims that love is all there is. Any negative feeling you may have is a lack of love. Give love to all around you. Be grateful and appreciate life. You will feel better. Rhonda Byrne also mentions to play games with your mind. That is what I did to help myself in my darkness. Games to help focus the mind work with discipline. We are all meant to be happy. Claim your happiness now. I feel I'm living proof of her book.

I think of positive thoughts like helium in a balloon. When enough helium goes into the balloon, the balloon begins to lift, and once the balloon stretches, it becomes easier to expand. The same principle applies regarding positive thoughts and feelings. With enough positivity inside us, our spirit lifts and we rise. After entering this higher plane, it's easier to keep afloat. All that's needed is a little force and focus to get started. To feel this elation is so worth the effort in the end. Asking the question "What would love do?" before making a decision helps point us in the right direction. That is the question God presents in Conversations with God. Then remember that love is kind. Love does not judge or control. Love has no need to be right. Love is all giving and forgiving. Love does not criticize. Love is not jealous. Love feels good.

Awareness of thought is the initial step. We are creating our world constantly, with awareness or without. If you plant crab apples, you can't expect to harvest golden delicious. That's all I'm saying. Once past the negatives in life, the experience of joy flows. Joy is possible for everyone. Only you can determine if you are willing to look inside yourself and do the work necessary to get to your joy, or as I call it, getting to the positive side of pain. All I know is that putting in the effort to go within myself is the best thing I have ever done.

There still remains one question that I'm not able to answer for myself. It's the question from the 'happiness survey' I started back in 2005. The question is: "Would you make the same decisions again now that you know the outcome?" I honestly am not able to answer that question. I hope I would make the same decisions in order to give my children the best life. However, knowing the consequence of those decisions, I'm not sure I would have the courage to walk into hell again. Even with knowing how Divine guidance delivered me this beautiful life now, I only hope I would choose the same path again. This I cannot say for sure.

What I *can* say is that I am grateful for my past now. Getting past the pain has given me strength and understanding. The joy I feel now is incredible. My positive feelings are so amplified that I find it hard to contain myself. Happiness is contagious, and I am on a mission to infest the world. Remember, wherever you go, *GO HAPPY!*

H*aving*
A*ll*
P*ower*
P*ropel*
Y*ou*

Several months ago I attended a retreat. One of the speakers noted that married women serve their husbands and single women serve God. I never heard that before, and it made me wonder. It's true I gave my life to God years ago but somehow I feel God has served me better than I've served Him. I often say the prayer I heard from Oprah, "Thank You for using me for something greater than myself." My hope is that this prayer will come to pass someday.

Wishing you the very best in life. Thank you for allowing me to share my journey with you. With love and gratitude I say, "All happiness to you!"

The Spirit Wind

Serenely blowing in the breeze
Quiet echoes in the trees
The Spirit wind touches our souls
And softly carries the voice of us all

Its natural force embraces
It's known to have many faces
The living source of life we know
Creates our world from the words we sow

Be careful what you say and do
Be certain your thoughts will carry you
The things we think, the things we say
All become real in some kind of way

Be careful what you say and do
Because it all will come back to you
Happy and free we are meant to be
Let it all go, and come fly with me

Terri's Birthday Dance 2011

CPSIA information can be obtained at www.ICGtesting.com
Printed in the USA
LVOW04s2152120914

403839LV00001B/3/P